WELCOME TO

THE REAL HISTORY

OF THE

CROWN

On 31 October 2016, Queen Elizabeth II became Britain's longest-reigning monarch, surpassing the record of 63 years, seven months and two days set by her great-grandmother, Queen Victoria. Later that same week, Netflix released *The Crown*, its tell-all biopic of the Queen's life, from her early marital conflicts to her fledgling years as a constitutional monarch. But how much of this award-winning drama is actually rooted in truth?

Over the following pages, go behind the palace doors and find out what life was really like for the Queen. Uncover the reality of Elizabeth's relationship with Philip Mountbatten, from the rifts and rumours that plagued their early marriage to their divided approach to parenthood and the lonely childhood of their first-born son, Prince Charles. Elsewhere, discover how romance ruined a king and paved the way for Elizabeth II, and find out what the Queen really thought about Britain's first female prime minister.

FUTURE

THE REAL HISTORY
OF THE
CROWN

Future PLC Quay House, The Ambury, Bath, BA1 1UA

Editorial
Editor **Philippa Grafton**
Designer **Andy Downes**
Compiled by **Jessica Leggett & Perry Wardell-Wicks**
Senior Art Editor **Andy Downes**
Head of Art & Design **Greg Whitaker**
Editorial Director **Jon White**

Cover images
Topfoto

Photography
All copyrights and trademarks are recognised and respected

Advertising
Media packs are available on request
Commercial Director **Clare Dove**

International
Head of Print Licensing **Rachel Shaw**
licensing@futurenet.com
www.futurecontenthub.com

Circulation
Head of Newstrade **Tim Mathers**

Production
Head of Production **Mark Constance**
Production Project Manager **Matthew Eglinton**
Advertising Production Manager **Joanne Crosby**
Digital Editions Controller **Jason Hudson**
Production Managers **Keely Miller, Nola Cokely,
Vivienne Calvert, Fran Twentyman**

Printed in the UK

Distributed by Marketforce, 5 Churchill Place, Canary Wharf, London, E14 5HU
www.marketforce.co.uk Tel: 0203 787 9001

The Real History of The Crown Seventh Edition (AHB4942)
© 2022 Future Publishing Limited

FUTURE Connectors.
Creators.
Experience
Makers.

Future plc is a public company quoted on the London Stock Exchange (symbol: FUTR)
www.futureplc.com

Chief executive **Zillah Byng-Thorne**
Non-executive chairman **Richard Huntingford**
Chief financial officer **Penny Ladkin-Brand**

Tel +44 (0)1225 442 244

Part of the

ALL ABOUT
HISTORY
bookazine series

Widely
Recycled

ipso. For press freedom
with responsibility

CONTENTS

22

8

122

82

110

100

116

62

HEAD

Royal biographer Robert Lacey reveals the truth behind the Queen's depiction, the royal scandals and marital strife in hit drama The Crown

Interview by **Dom Reseigh-Lincoln** and **Jessica Leggett**

While royal period dramas are commonplace, few have attempted to depict the life of a reigning monarch. But this is exactly what hit Netflix drama *The Crown* does, portraying the early years of Queen Elizabeth II following her ascent to the British throne.

Set from 1947 to 1955, *The Crown*'s first season tackled some of the most influential moments in the young queen's life, from the untimely death of her father, George VI, to the public scandal of her sister's love affair. It also touches on other key events like Winston Churchill's re-election, Cold War tensions and even the Great Smog of London. Series two delved further into Palace scandals and the family's evolving relationships.

The show has always courted controversy (and critical acclaim) because it doesn't shy away from the Queen's relationship with Prince Philip, played in the first two series by Claire Foy and Matt Smith, respectively. This ranges from their early passion to the strains the monarchy has put on their marriage as Elizabeth is forced to make tough choices and Philip becomes sidelined.

The Crown has been created by Peter Morgan, who also wrote the Oscar-winning movie *The Queen*. The show has been given a similar Hollywood treatment, with a rumoured £100 million spent on its lavish production design and costumes. But how much dramatic license has been taken with facts to ensure its as gripping as you average blockbuster?

Back in 2019, we spoke to Robert Lacey, one of the Queen's official biographers and a consultant on the show, about its accuracy.

How did you become involved with *The Crown*?

In 1977, I wrote a book called *Majesty* that looked at the role of the monarchy in the political system and the national imagination. After Diana's death, the royal family had their greatest crisis of all and I interviewed a number of people who were at Buckingham Palace and Balmoral at the time.

Because of my research, Peter Morgan asked me to help with his first film, *The Queen*, and since then we've worked on *The Audience* together. He then asked me to get involved in helping with the historical accuracy of his new show, *The Crown*.

As a historical consultant, I'm involved with the words in the scripts, which is really interesting - especially as there are two dramatic centres in the [first] series. Although it starts with a royal date, 1947, it finishes with the retirement of Winston Churchill in 1955 with a mixture of royal and political in between. I should stress that there is a huge research team working behind the scenes, not just me, and they all do a wonderful job.

While it's very much based on a real story, do you feel the show has taken creative licence with the royals?

Well, you'd expect me to say that, but the way I try and describe it is that every single incident you see is based on very thorough historical research. While there are moments when drama departs from dry history and imagines what someone would have done in these situations, there are wonderful, obscure facts that a lot people couldn't believe when they saw the show. For example, there really was a pet raven hopping around while Elizabeth was having her constitutional history lessons.

I interviewed people who had been taught by Doctor Marten [Elizabeth's private tutor as a child, seen in flashbacks] and they remember him feeding this raven sugar lumps, so it's a mixture of very thorough research to create details like that you wouldn't quite think true. On the other hand, when it comes to something like the Great Smog of London, Churchill's secretary who died in the smog is an invention - but she's based on all of the secretaries who ever worked for Churchill. The thing about drama is that it gives that leap of imagination that transports you to being there.

How true to life is the show's portrayal of Philip and Elizabeth's relationship?

One of the things I really like about the show is the way in which it depicts the marriage as a love match. The fact that Elizabeth did have to fight back against her family who were very uncertain about this prickly, European prince - who, of course gave up his title for the first ten years of the reign. It's something that Elizabeth has never shied away from.

Her father's official biography says that this is the man that she has been in love with since

"THERE ARE WONDERFUL, OBSCURE FACTS"

Claire Foy won numerous awards for her performance

The Crown explores the highs and lows of the Queen and Prince Philip's relationship

Depicting Elizabeth's close relationship with her father was a clear goal for The Crown

their first meeting when she was 13. Those words could only have been written with her approval, so we know he was right for her from the beginning.

It's fascinating how *The Crown* shows how Elizabeth came to the throne as a Mountbatten. When she married Philip in 1947, the topic of her surname was of great importance. They looked in the House of Windsor Act but nothing was mentioned about a surname, so she came to the throne as Elizabeth Mountbatten.

We even see a true depiction of the moment Lord Mountbatten lifts a glass and says, "House Mountbatten rules". It was only a few weeks after that it was decided she should be called Windsor. Again, it's one of those obscure details but it's absolutely true and it brings out the drama between this young married couple.

The Crown shows how close Elizabeth was to her father, George VI. How did this relationship help shape her?
Elizabeth was incredibly close to her father and took such inspiration from him. She did, after all, give up the idea of having a large family after her first two children and didn't resume for another ten years. It really shows her sense of duty and priorities as a princess and a queen-in-waiting.

"IT'S EQUALLY ABOUT THE POLITICS TAKING PLACE IN DOWNING STREET"

The Crown really captures that clash between personal connection and duty. One of the key reasons that the Queen has maintained her legacy for so many decades has been her sense of duty - but that has been at the cost of her family. We see her emotional life being stunted by not being able to say the first things that come to her heart. She always has to ponder everything. As the show goes on, we're going to see the personal penalties she and the royal family have to pay for having to live a life of duty.

How big a scandal was Princess Margaret's affair with Peter Townsend in real life?
The Crown really does bring out the hypocrisy of the government's attitude at the time with the subject of Townsend wanting to divorce his wife for Margaret. The prime minister at the time, Anthony

Eden, was a divorced man but that didn't prevent him from fulfilling his role and blockading the union. In a later season of *The Crown*, [we see] the legacy of this situation with the rise of Harold Wilson and the changes that he makes to divorce laws - something that Margaret and her future husband, Antony Armstrong-Jones, take advantage of in 1960.

I think the show does a wonderful job of showing how the Queen is torn between the love for her sister - wanting to give Margaret what she wants so badly and giving her compensation for being the sibling of a monarch - but is ultimately prevented by the politicians. What really happened was that Eden and the Cabinet said that after the age of 25, Margaret was free to marry Townsend if she so wished, but there would be no pension or financial support. It was an incredibly tense situation for all involved.

SECRET SCANDALS
OF THE
ROYAL FAMILY

Uncover five scandals that stayed out of the British press - at least for a time...

King Edward VIII in crown crisis

Edward VIII caused a constitutional crisis when he abdicated to marry American divorcée Wallis Simpson. Their relationship had been widely reported in America and Europe but the British press chose to ignore it. They hid the extent of the affair until 1936, when it became clear that the king would rather give up his crown than his mistress.

Edward VIII's murderous mistress

One of the most successful cover-ups of the 1920s revolved around Edward and his first mistress, Maggie Alibert. Having murdered her husband, Maggie's trial was all over the papers but her affair with Edward was kept under wraps. She also used sordid letters from Edward to blackmail her way to freedom and was acquitted of all charges.

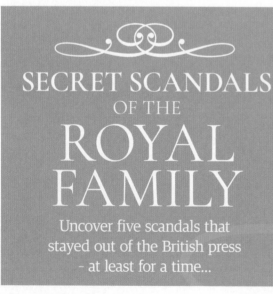

© Alamy

Princess Margaret's affair with Peter Townsend features prominently in the series

Through flashbacks, we get to see the fallout of the abdication crisis

How does Winston Churchill's return to power fit into the story?

There was a great deal of sentimentality on Churchill's part of this beautiful young queen, of this second Elizabethan age and of that fact he couldn't quite believe he was back in power after his first tenure as prime minister in 1940-45. I think one of the strengths of [series one] is that it's set in two places. A lot of the story takes place in Buckingham Palace but it's equally about the politics taking place in Downing Street.

I think the drama and the appeal of the show is as much the political side of it as the one involving the royals. It gives a way to not just enjoy seeing great characters, such as Churchill, but also the big events to come, like Britain's role in the world, the changing economy and beyond. We worked very hard to ensure these social changes were all accurately reflected in *The Crown*.

Do you know if the Queen or other members of the royal family have seen the show?

I don't believe the Queen herself would be concerned with watching something like *The Crown*, but we do know that some people close to her have seen it and, as far as we're aware, have enjoyed and liked it. Sadly, that can't be taken as any sort of royal approval.

The official Palace line on the series is that it's a work of 'fiction' and it's not going to comment on anything that's deemed as such, but I think that's just bucking the issue, really. It is certainly fiction in the sense that it's a TV drama, but it is still based on a real history and we're very proud of how accurate we've been with the facts. Part of the show's appeal is that we've stayed true to the actual events and that's made *The Crown* so popular and such a success.

All four series of *The Crown* are available on Blu-ray, DVD and Platinum Edition Blu-ray and DVD, courtesy of Sony Pictures Home Entertainment. *The Crown: The Inside History*, written by Robert Lacey and published by Blink Publishing, is currently available from all good book shops RRP £20.

The tragic tale of Prince John

The youngest child of King George V and Queen Mary, Prince John, was kept hidden from the public for most of his life. He suffered from epilepsy, which most likely contributed to his severe learning disabilities. He was moved away to Sandringham House with only a governess for company and died from a severe seizure in 1919, aged just 13.

Princess Margaret and the bank job

The 2008 film *The Bank Job* suggests that a 1971 raid on a London bank was actually a secret service cover-up to secure lurid photos of Princess Margaret. The alleged scandal is hotly contested, though the government did mysteriously impose a gagging order, a D-notice, to prevent any news coverage of the robbery.

The Queen's drug-addicted uncle

George, Duke of Kent, descended into drug addiction under the influence of one of his lovers, Kiki Preston. His hedonistic lifestyle was covered up, even after his tragic death in a plane crash in 1942 at the age of 39. It was not until a 2003 documentary, *The Queen's Lost Uncle*, that George was brought to mainstream attention.

In a break from royal protocol, Edward VIII and his mistress, Wallis Simpson, watch the royal proclamation ceremony from a window in St James's Palace in 1936

THE FAMILY SHAME

The family's black sheep, Edward VIII ascended the throne to great fanfare but felt compelled to give it up within a year, and died a friendless exile with a ruined reputation

Words by **James Price**

"I have found it impossible to carry the heavy burden of responsibility and to discharge my duties as king as I would wish to do without the help and support of the woman I love... And now, we all have a new king. I wish him and you, his people, happiness and prosperity with all my heart. God bless you all! God save the king!"

With these final words, broadcast over BBC radio on 11 December 1936 at Windsor Castle, the man who had until recently been Edward VIII announced to his former subjects that he had abdicated as king in favour of his younger brother following a tumultuous end to his 325-day reign.

The former king returned to his family, kissing them goodbye and sharing a farewell drink with his brothers. As he left, he bowed to Bertie, the younger brother who had succeeded him, and headed off to Portsmouth, where a Royal Navy destroyer was waiting to take him away from the country he had once ruled.

Once the wildly popular King Edward VIII and the shining beacon of hope for the British Empire, he would never feel welcome in Britain again and would live the rest of his life a tragic and somewhat embarrassing outcast of the royal family in effective exile. And the reason he felt compelled to surrender the throne he had been born and raised to sit on, risking constitutional crisis and division across a global empire, was that he wished to marry a divorced woman.

As hard as it is to understand today, the United Kingdom's divorce laws at the time were strict. As the Church of England did not approve of divorce, divorcees were forbidden in law to remarry while their former partner lived. Edward, who as monarch was also the head of the Church of England (ironically the result of Henry VIII's determination to end his own marriage) was as bound to this law as any other. In seeking to marry Wallis Simpson, who had already left one husband and was in the midst of a second divorce, Edward put himself on a collision course with an inflexible church, a disapproving government and many of his subjects.

This decision, taken for love, changed the course of the monarchy and split the royal family - it led to a man who was at first treated with adulation being shunned by his family, driven from his home, kept away from family occasions and having his wife - whose biggest crime was getting divorced - ignored and looked down upon by generations of the royal family.

But despite this tragic story having all the ingredients to be the greatest romantic act of the 20th century, Edward VIII's legacy has become shrouded in sinister suspicions - of extremist political views, ties to Nazism and even suggestions he was the 'traitor king', prepared to be Hitler's puppet in order to regain the throne he'd felt compelled to leave.

The man who ruled for just 325 days has cast a large and menacing shadow over the Windsor dynasty and continues to draw significant debate and interest today. But how did it come to this?

Edward Albert Christian George Andrew Patrick David, or simply David to his family, was not always doomed to tragic failure. Having served during World War I and conducted himself admirably during globe-trotting tours of the British Empire, he was hugely popular in Britain as well as abroad. He also won support for his tours of deprived areas of Britain to champion the common people, and his support for back-to-work schemes. With flair, modernism, good looks and

WHO WAS WALLIS?

At one point the most infamous woman in the world, how much is known of the real Wallis?

Wallis Simpson was not a typical candidate to be a future Queen. Having grown up far from European royal courts, she was raised in challenging circumstances in Maryland, USA. Her father died when she was very young, leaving her mother to work odd jobs, sell needlework and take in lodgers in order to make ends meet, as well as receive occasional support from wealthy relatives.

She was married to a naval pilot named Lieutenant Win Spencer in 1916, but their marriage was pock-marked with long absences from one another, as his military duties took him across the US and eventually to the Far East. Wallis later followed him there and toured China, exposing her to much of the European colonial society there. The marriage was not a happy one, and by 1927 she was in the process of her first divorce when she met Ernest Simpson, a well-off British-American shipping magnate, in New York. Perhaps giving an insight into her priorities at the time (like many socially mobile people of the period), she was far from head over heels but saw Ernest as a solid bet, noting that he was "kind and good-looking" to her mother, according to Anne Sebba. Ernest swiftly fell in love with Wallis and almost as swiftly divorced his then-wife Dorothea in order to marry Wallis in 1928. The couple soon moved to Britain and found themselves, through mutual acquaintances, in the inner circle of the heir to the throne.

Was Wallis an ambitious schemer who was prepared to destroy an empire in order to get a foot up in society? It is doubtful, as she clearly made efforts to break out of the relationship in those crucial months at the end of 1936. More likely she was ambitious and was excited by the attentions of a prince and then a king.

She also kept in contact with Ernest even as she divorced him. One letter from 1937 confides, "Wherever you are, you can be sure that never a day goes by without some hours' thought of you," while another from 1936 laments, "Wasn't life lovely, sweet and simple," she wrote. "I can't believe that such a thing could have happened to two people who got along so well – at least it never should have been like it is now." That she still had feelings for her husband even as she filed for divorce hints at either an emotionally confused or highly ambitious person – though which is the real Wallis Simpson is impossible to say for sure – if either.

Wallis was remarked to be not particularly attractive or talented, but she was clearly magnetic to Edward

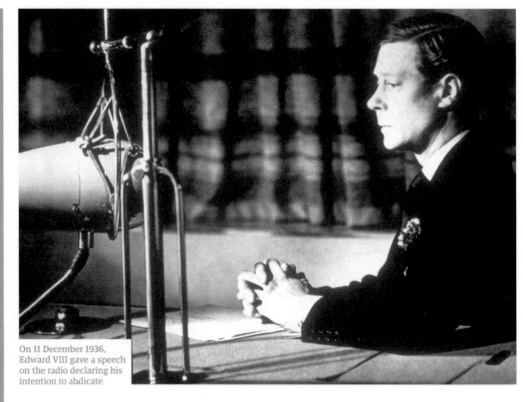

On 11 December 1936, Edward VIII gave a speech on the radio declaring his intention to abdicate

charisma, he won attention and acclaim the world over. He was, according to historian Michael Bloch, "the idol of all classes, built up by the press and official propaganda into an almost godlike figure."

But the Prince of Wales, as he was then, also quickly developed a reputation as a playboy. He surrounded himself with a close circle that largely came from outside court life. His more flamboyant attitudes drew the ire of conservative establishment figures, not least Alan 'Tommy' Lascelles, the future private secretary to George VI and Elizabeth II, who remarked in 1927, "I can't help thinking that the best thing that could happen to him and the country, would be for him to break his neck." It is also telling that this was said to Prime Minister Stanley Baldwin, who agreed with Lascelles' sentiment.

The prince had a penchant for married women, and had several affairs with prominent socialites, including Freda Dudley Ward and Thelma, Viscount Furness, an American married to a British nobleman. The prince was a fan of all things American, so Lady Furness introduced him to British-American businessman Ernest Simpson and his American wife, Wallis, in 1931. The couple soon joined the prince's inner circle, but by 1934 it was clear that Wallis had come to be a great deal more than a mere friend. The clouds of constitutional crisis were already looming over the prince's head.

As a once-divorced and currently married American woman of no significant wealth or family pedigree, it is unsurprising that the Prince of Wales's choice of companion did not meet with approval. His father, a stern disciplinarian, was said to be particularly disapproving of his son's infatuation with Wallis, and believed his son's

rejection of his 'duty' to marry and settle down with someone suitable was a sure sign of Edward's unsuitability to rule: "After I am dead, the boy will ruin himself within 12 months," he is prophetically quoted as saying.

But despite this disapproval – or perhaps even because of it, as he had a strained relationship with his father – Edward drew Wallis closer to him, and in 1935 dropped all pretence of secrecy, openly holidaying with her and taking her on tours without her husband. Wallis was said to have treated Edward poorly – he would lavish her

Elizabeth Taylor sits with Wallis at a party in Paris in the 1960s. The royal couple had moved to Paris after the abdication crisis

The Duke and Duchess of Windsor enjoy time together during their time in the Bahamas, safely away from events in Europe

with gifts and she in turn would talk down to him and show him little respect. She referred to him in letters to Ernest as 'Peter Pan' - the boyish prince who wouldn't grow up. This did little to endear her to the courtiers, but such a free attitude in a constrained world was one of the alluring aspects of Wallis to Edward's eyes. According to Bloch, "There is no doubt that his lonely nature found in her a spiritual comradeship... he felt that he and Mrs Simpson were made for each other." That he was obsessed with her was all too apparent. According to historian Anna Pasternak, courtiers remarked how he was "exalté to the point of madness."

Edward was sheltered from public scrutiny in Britain by a gentlemen's agreement between the press and the royal family to not report personal dealings. So despite his questionable personal dealings and increasing concern from courtiers that the prince was more concerned with his social life than royal duties, he remained hugely popular among all classes of British society.

But while the masses worshipped the prince, he himself had misgivings, and writing in 1950 in *Life* magazine claims to have discussed with his brothers the possibility of abdicating the throne once their father died as early as 1935.

"EDWARD WAS SHELTERED FROM PUBLIC SCRUTINY IN BRITAIN"

The prince could hide from his responsibilities no longer when George V died, and the Prince of Wales became King Edward VIII on 20 January 1936. Edward's account of the immediate aftermath of his father's death reveals how unprepared mentally he was for his new role: "While my mind was still trying to comprehend the profound event that had in that instant occurred, my mother did an unexpected thing. She took my hand in hers and kissed it; before I could stop him my brother George, who was standing beside her, stepped forward and followed her example. The action embarrassed me."

Edward VIII's reign was brief, riven with divisions and uncertainty. He immediately broke convention by watching the proclamation of his accession to the throne from the window of St James's Palace - with Wallis Simpson beside him. He also set about making cuts in the royal

household. This could have been a modernising act, as the country still reeled from the Great Depression, but while he made these cuts to jobs and salaries he also lavished Wallis with gifts. This did nothing to endear either of them to the household.

Edward was also reluctant to discuss his coronation - a hugely important ceremony. His reason for wishing to avoid it was, he later wrote, because it was a sacred ritual, and he could not face "being crowned with a lie on my lips." He would not cross the line, as he saw it, that would make him king before God. The lie he referred to, of course, was his intention to marry Wallis Simpson.

Wallis herself, it seems, attempted multiple times to halt the divorce. In private letters, she yearns to be out of the situation: "I really must return to Ernest... I am sure you and I would only

Images © Getty

create disaster together," she wrote to the king in October 1936.

However, Edward would not accept any suggestion of separation, even threatening to kill himself if she left him, according to some accounts. "At the time of the abdication, Edward slept with a loaded gun under his pillow and threatened to kill himself if Wallis forsook him," Pasternak reported. Whether he went to this extreme or not, Edward himself acknowledges that Wallis tried to leave him. Again writing in *Life* in 1950, he recalled how Wallis had messaged him to say, "'Under no circumstances was I to give up the throne'. Even had she been able to make herself understood, her plea would not have diverted me from my determined course... in the desperate hope of staying the abdication she had, alone, decided to leave me." Wallis, whatever her original intentions, faced no escape.

When Wallis obtained the first stage of her divorce from the court in October 1936, Edward confronted Prime Minister Baldwin, expressing his intentions. "Marriage had become an indispensable condition to my continued existence, whether as king or as man... If I could marry her as king, all well and good. I would be happy and in consequence a better king. But if, on the other hand, the Government opposed the marriage... then I was prepared to go," he declared.

Several alternatives were proposed by the king and his advisors: Winston Churchill advocated delay. A morganatic marriage was also put forward - where Wallis would be his wife but not queen - but Baldwin's cabinet rejected this.

Baldwin laid out the options to the king: abandon the marriage; abdicate the throne; or insist on marriage and have the entire government resign - bringing to a head a constitutional crisis.

The duke and duchess defied British government advice when they toured Nazi Germany in 1937, which included a two-hour meeting with Hitler himself

"EDWARD THREATENED TO KILL HIMSELF IF SHE LEFT HIM"

Edward was not deterred: "If the real intention was to scare me into giving up Wallis by pointing at my head this big pistol of the Government's threatened resignation they had clearly misjudged their man," he later explained.

And so Edward made the decision to abdicate the throne he had been raised to warm, in favour of his "untrained, reluctant and embarrassed successor of far less obvious gifts," as Bloch summarised. Edward signed the papers of abdication at Fort Belvedere on 10 December 1936 in the presence of his brothers.

The public were dismayed: kept in the dark until just a few days before abdication, opinion

THE MARBURG FILES

Buried Nazi documents recovered in 1945 revealed information on Germany's secret plans for the duke and duchess

In May 1945 Allied forces captured a German translator, who took them to a store of secret Nazi documents. Most Nazi paperwork had been hastily destroyed, so its survival was remarkable. Years later, when it was checked by British, French and American historians, a file on the duke and duchess came to light – the Marburg Files. And the contents were explosive.

They detailed telegrams pertaining to the couple and reported conversations, in which the duke was dismissive of the war effort and the chances of British victory. One such conversation was with a Spanish diplomat. According to historian Karina Urbach, Don Javier Bermejillo

reported the duke blaming "the Jews, the Reds and the Foreign Office for the war". In a conversation on 25 June 1940, "Bermejillo reported that Windsor stressed if one bombed England effectively this could bring peace," according to Urbach.

Details were also passed on of conversations about the duke returning to the British throne, but the duke replied that it was constitutionally impossible after an abdication. "When [an] agent then remarked the course of war may produce changes even in the British constitution the duchess in particular became very thoughtful."

This also tied in with details of a plot, named Operation Willi, in which

the Germans planned to kidnap or persuade the couple to stay in Madrid instead of sailing to the Bahamas, and there be induced to retake the throne with German help, or force a peace with Britain.

Churchill, who heard of the files' existence, worked to have all the documents destroyed, but copies had already been made and sent to the US. He instead persuaded the Americans to not publish, dismissing the entire thing as "tendentious and unreliable". The US president agreed, stating they were "obviously concocted with some idea of promoting German propaganda and weakening western resistance" and were "totally unfair."

Their trip to Germany in 1937 convinced high-ranking Nazis of their willingness to aid Germany during WWII

In 1967, the Duke and Duchess of Windsor were invited to celebrate the centenary of the birth of Edward's mother, Queen Mary

was bitterly divided. Some saw in it a tragedy that inflexible systems and an uncompromising government had forced out the rightful ruler; others saw an unforgivable dereliction of duty. Wallis Simpson became a schemer who tore an empire apart in many eyes.

Had Edward used Wallis as an excuse to escape the responsibility of being king? It is hotly contested, though his determination to marry Wallis whatever the cost suggests that this alone was his aim. Edward, to no great surprise, argued it was both love and duty that drove him: "I certainly married because I chose the path of love, but I abdicated because I chose the path of duty. I did not value the crown so lightly that I gave it away hastily. I valued it so deeply I surrendered it rather than risk any impairment of its prestige."

Edward, so wrapped up in trying to secure his marriage, had made little thought of where he would go next. His demands had been to get Wallis's divorce sorted immediately (which did not occur), to be allowed to return to Fort Belvedere, the one place he considered home (he was not, despite his brother's promise) and to be given a pension (which he received, despite already amassing money for this very moment).

Edward - who was made Duke of Windsor - left for the continent. The globe-spanning empire of 500 million people was still simply not large enough for two kings, so he headed to Austria to be reunited with Wallis. There they waited for five months for her divorce, and finally wed on 3 June 1937 in France - though no members of the royal family were in attendance.

That George VI did not attend is no huge surprise, but the absence of any of the family illustrates the growing discord. It had been assumed by many, not least the duke, that he would be able to return to Britain and the royal family within a few years and take on a junior position. Even in 1938, Prime Minister Neville Chamberlain argued: "The right course was for the Duke of Windsor to be treated as soon as possible as a younger brother of the king who could take some of the royal functions off his brother's hands," according to Bloch.

But relations became increasingly strained. Resentment bubbled away in the royal family, who disliked the duke's attempts to squeeze money from them and live a celebrity lifestyle, while convictions hardened - particularly in his mother - that the duke had turned his back on his duty to

family and country. The Duke of Windsor, on the other hand, was bitterly wounded by the king's refusal to bestow the name 'Her Royal Highness' on Wallis. It was a sore point that rankled for the rest of the duke's life.

It was this lack of proper respect, according to the duke, that led the couple in 1937 to commit another controversial act - a tour of Nazi Germany and a meeting with Hitler. This act and the couple's political outlook has divided historians ever since. Were they Nazi supporters? Writer Andrew Morton argues that the real reason for the tour "was to show Wallis a good time and see exactly what it was like to enjoy a royal tour." The couple were curtsied to, cheered and called 'Your Royal Highness' at every opportunity. But was that the only reason for the visit?

The Duke of Windsor, following his abdication, for the first time in his life had no direction or place in the world. That he was trying to stay relevant and carve out a role for himself on the global stage is clear. But there is also a significant body of evidence suggesting the duke was also, if not a full-blown Nazi, then sympathetic.

The duke's political opinions are mired in mystery. While many historians, such as Carolyn

Harris, argue that the visit to Germany was because the duke "seems to have envisioned a diplomatic role for himself as a mediator between Britain and Germany," others argue it was a sign of his political allegiances. Morton says, "he was certainly sympathetic... even after the war he thought Hitler was a good fellow and that he'd done a good job in Germany, and he was also anti-Semitic, before, during and after the war." These opinions have been fuelled by quotes attributed to Hitler himself by the likes of the less-than-trustworthy Nazi Albert Speer. He reported Hitler saying, "If [the duke] had stayed, everything would have been different. His abdication was a severe loss for us." Released FBI files also suggest the duchess was in a relationship with Joachim von Ribbentrop, the Nazi foreign minister, and later passed him sensitive information.

But whatever the real reasons for the visit, it has tarnished his reputation and haunted his legacy. The tragic king was to become the traitor king because of this association.

It seems evident, however, that the duke wanted peace, almost at any cost. Having witnessed the horrors of WWI, he was far from alone in wanting to avoid conflict. The policy of appeasement towards the Nazis by the British in the 1930s was pursued almost until the declaration of war. In 1939 the duke took to the radio to broadcast a message of peace. Whether the duke continued to work towards this end even during the war is suggested. Secret Nazi files uncovered after WWII revealed documents about the Windsors suggesting they were critical of the war and supportive of peace with Germany.

At the outbreak of war the duke and duchess had been residing in France. The duke promptly offered his services as a go-between for the British and French militaries. Upon the German conquest, the couple headed to fascist Madrid, before being encouraged on to neutral but British-friendly Portugal. With rumours circulating about the duke and duchess's political affinities, as well as the couple being dangerously exposed on the continent, Churchill hatched a plan to send the duke to govern the Bahamas.

The duke was far from delighted by this suggestion, and his reluctance even reportedly prompted Churchill to threaten him with court martial. The duke finally relented, and remained in the Bahamas from August 1940 until the end of the war. The duchess was said to call it "our St Helena" in reference to the tiny, remote island Napoleon Bonaparte had been exiled to. For them it was not a chance to serve in part of the British Empire: it was a banishment.

Following the conclusion of WWII, the duke resigned as governor and returned to Europe. But the time apart and the strains of war did not make a family reunion any more likely. Hoping to get a position as a diplomat of sorts between Britain and the US in 1945, his hopes were dashed as the royal family remained distant. Whether his apparent Nazi sympathies bred resentment and

The couple were finally able to marry on 3 June 1937, which also just happened to be his father George V's birthday – the same father who was vocal in his disapproval of Wallis Simpson

The duke and duchess were deeply attached to their pugs, which were reportedly ill-trained and indulged

DAILY EXPRESS, Thursday, Dec. 3, 1936.

Buying
Christmas gifts today?
Choose —

Bear Brand

Hose in boxes gay

Daily Express

TODAY'S WEATHER: CLOUDY; UNSETTLED.

RADIO PROGRAMMES: PAGE 23.

No. 11,405

THURSDAY, DECEMBER 3, 1936

ONE PENNY

YOU OWE IT TO YOUR FAMILY

to secure for them and for yourself the protection of the Daily Express Free Family Insurance Policy.

Register with your newsagent **today**.

THE KING AND HIS MINISTERS

Constitutional Crisis

AT No. 10 LAST NIGHT

Mollison Missing

CABINET ADVICE

AN ACUTE CONSTITUTIONAL CRISIS HAS ARISEN BETWEEN THE KING AND HIS MINISTERS.

The King has intimated that he wishes to make a marriage. The Cabinet have advised against this course.

Mr Baldwin, the Prime Minister, saw the King at Buckingham Palace last night. He remained with him for just over an hour. After his departure the King left the Palace, alone, in his car.

Mr Baldwin returned to his room at the House of Commons and conferred with some of his colleagues for an hour and a half, then went to No. 10, Downing St. Shortly after nine o'clock Sir John Simon, the Home Secretary, arrived for a consultation with him. He

LIGHTED WINDOWS OF NO. 10 DOWNING ST—THE PRIME MINISTER'S HOME—DURING THE CONSULTATION, LAST NIGHT, BETWEEN MR BALDWIN AND HIS HOME SECRETARY SIR JOHN SIMON.

Much of the build-up to the abdication crisis was played out in private in Britain, until the final ten days - when supporters of the king and government raced to sway public opinion

PRAYERS OFFERED

PRAYERS WERE OFFERED IN VILLAGES AND TOWNS ON THE COAST SOUTH OF CAPETOWN LAST NIGHT WHEN THE NEWS WAS BROKEN THAT JIM MOLLISON WAS MISSING ON HIS VAIN ATTEMPT TO BEAT THE LONDON-CAPE AIR RECORD.

Flying with a leaking petrol tank, Mollison and co-pilot Molinier left Kimberley.

—**2,145,000**—

New Record

Last week the net sale of the Daily Express reached a new high record.

STOP PRESS

TWO INJURED IN

"HE REMAINED ON BAD TERMS WITH HIS MOTHER"

mistrust, it is not entirely clear, although King George VI was said to have read the Marburg Files: Sir Alexander Cardigan revealed the king "fussed about the Duke of Windsor's file and the captured German documents," according to Bloch.

The duke and duchess remained in temporary and borrowed homes in France, entertaining guests and hosting parties. But it was far from a stimulating existence, and the duke tried and failed repeatedly to weave a path back into the royal family. Not even the peacetime leadership of Churchill in 1951 brought a reconciliation. The duke's most notable returns to Britain were to attend the funerals of his family - starting with his brother and king, George VI, in 1952.

Following George's death, Elizabeth ascended the throne, although again this did not precipitate a reconciliation. The duke even stayed away from the coronation, conveniently arguing that a former sovereign was not a fit guest at the ceremony.

He remained on particularly bad terms with his mother, who had been badly affected by losing three of her sons - and despising a fourth. The antipathy was mutual, and when the duke returned to Britain for her funeral in 1953, the words he wrote to Wallis, who was forbidden from coming, were far from heartbroken: "I'm afraid her veins have always been as icy cold as they are in death." This bitterness was extended to the rest of his family: "What a smug stinking lot my relations are, and you've never seen such a seedy worn-out bunch of old hags most of them have become."

Following his brother's death the duke seems to have become resigned to his state of exile, and the couple finally bought their own property in France. The duke and duchess were called 'Your Royal Highness' and the servants wore royal livery. The duke spent much of his time writing his memoirs and articles for magazines. He never held an official office again.

As news broke of constitutional crisis, spontaneous support erupted for the king

There were small moments of reconciliation - both he and the duchess were invited to Britain in 1967 to attend the unveiling of a plaque to the duke's mother. It was a gesture made by the Queen, though the Queen Mother was notably absent, having also grown to detest the duke and duchess. Clearly there was too much bad blood to ever heal these wounds within the family.

The duke died of throat cancer in France on 28 May 1972 at the age of 77. He was visited in his final days by Queen Elizabeth - another final gesture of reconciliation. He was finally to return to Britain after death, and was buried in the royal cemetery near Windsor Castle. Wallis, the woman the duke chose over a throne, was to join him there 14 years later.

The funeral of the Duke of Windsor

In an unexpected twist of compassion, the Duke of Windsor was laid to rest in his home country – although unlike other sovereigns of Great Britain, Edward is buried in the Royal Burial Ground at Frogmore. His service, held in St George's Chapel where his body lay in state for three days, was attended by the royal family, as well as the infamous Duchess of Windsor. Wallis, then aged 75, was invited to stay at Buckingham Palace but was noticeably frail and showing signs of the dementia that would consume her in her later years. She travelled back to Paris after the funeral.

— 5 June 1972 —

Princess Elizabeth hard at work at her studies at Windsor Castle in June 1940

TO TEACH A
QUEEN

An heir's education has always been a serious matter, but Elizabeth's parents decided to prioritise a happy childhood over preparation for the daunting task of ruling

Words by **Melanie Clegg**

Throughout history, the education of the heir to the throne has always been a matter of paramount importance, with huge amounts of attention paid to ensuring that the heir in question receives not just the best education possible but also a proper preparation for the gruelling task ahead.

In the 16th century, the children of Henry VIII had been provided with extraordinarily thorough educations that encompassed several languages as well as mathematics, philosophy and theology. In the 19th century, Queen Victoria and Prince Albert had taken an intense interest in the training of their eldest son, Bertie, Prince of Wales, creating a strict educational regimen that had covered a broad range of subjects and ensured that their son was, albeit rather unwillingly, one of the best educated monarchs ever to succeed to the British throne. Unfortunately, Bertie's experience had been such a miserable one that he had decided not to repeat it when it came to his own children, whose own education was relatively unremarkable and in some respects rather desultory considering their station. To the horror of Queen Victoria, both

of her eldest grandsons, Prince Albert Victor and Prince George, who would succeed as George V in 1911, struggled to speak any languages other than English, and attempts to force them to improve their linguistic skills were destined to fail horribly. In contrast, George's wife, Mary, was exceptionally well educated and was able to speak not just French and German but also some Italian, thanks to a year spent in Florence as a young woman. It was due to her that the next generation of royals, which included her sons Edward VIII and George VI, was rather better educated.

When Mary's granddaughter Elizabeth was born in April 1926, she was not expected to ever succeed to the throne. Her father's elder brother, David, Prince of Wales, was still only in his early 30s and although he had not yet married, it was naturally anticipated that he would do so very soon and then commence producing his own brood of children. Thus, Elizabeth's parents felt no great pressure to impose a rigorous education upon their daughter, preferring instead to emulate the cheerfully undemanding upbringing that her mother, the Duchess of York, had enjoyed as the youngest daughter of a Scottish earl.

In common with other upper-class girls of the time, the Duchess of York had, except for a brief spell at an exclusive school in London, been educated at home by a series of governesses, who taught her French and some German and encouraged an early passion for history. Although some upper-class girls were sent to boarding school, it was still considered the norm for them to be educated at home, while their brothers, who were deemed more in need of a proper education, were sent away to school, followed by university.

When Queen Mary expressed some concern about the education of Elizabeth and her younger sister Margaret – who was born in 1930 but didn't join her in the schoolroom until the age of seven – the Duchess of York airily dismissed her worries by reminding her that her own parents had considered it far more important to prepare their daughters to make good marriages, and that this gamble had definitely paid off, as "I and my sisters all married well, some of us very well". As far as the Duchess was concerned, there was no reason for her own daughters to be educated any differently, especially as it was so unlikely that either of them would be succeeding to the throne.

Art was a favourite pastime of both of the sisters, although neither had any particular talent

"SHE WAS TAKEN ABACK BY HOW UNDEMANDING THE ROYAL FAMILY WERE"

They were instead almost certainly destined to marry into the upper echelons of the aristocracy, where they would be fully employed running great houses, overseeing huge households and raising their own children.

As soon as she was born, Elizabeth, who would be known as 'Lilibet' in tribute to her initial attempts to pronounce her own name, was consigned to the devoted care of her mother's old nanny, the redoubtable Clara Knight, known as 'Allah' by her young charges, who adored her. Allah was the archetypical formidable British nanny, who ran the nursery with a strict attention to detail, ensuring that every moment of Elizabeth's day was fully accounted for and that there were no opportunities for idleness, fidgeting or bad behaviour. Meals were plain and wholesome, toys were played with one at a time and then carefully put away, there was a daily walk whatever the weather and the highlight of every day was the precious hour spent downstairs with her parents every evening before she was whisked away to bed in the nursery.

However, although Allah ruled the nursery, it was the Duchess of York herself who taught Elizabeth to read and encouraged her to embark on a lifelong love of books, which had the additional benefit of enabling her to remedy any deficiencies in her education. "I read quite quickly now," Elizabeth would tell the author JK Rowling many years later. "I have to read a lot."

When her younger sister Margaret was born, Allah took charge of the new baby while Elizabeth was passed to the care of a new nanny, Margaret 'Bobo' MacDonald, who would remain with her for the rest of her life as dresser and confidante, touchingly always referring to Elizabeth as her 'little lady' even after she had become Queen.

In 1933, when Elizabeth was seven years old, the York nursery upstairs in their town house at 145 Piccadilly was joined by a bright new Scottish governess, Marion Crawford, who was quickly nicknamed 'Crawfie' by her charges. She would supervise the education of the two princesses, aided by a series of tutors for French, dancing, music and art - all of which were considered essential accomplishments for upper class girls. Crawfie was rather taken aback by how undemanding the royal family were about her charges' educations, writing later in her controversial book *The Little Princesses* that "no one ever had employers who interfered so little." She confided that their gruff grandfather, who adored Elizabeth and treated her with a warm-hearted affection that he had rarely shown to his own children, had cornered her in order to demand: "For goodness sake, teach Margaret and Lilibet a decent hand, that's all I ask of you." George V's own handwriting was execrable, while his terrible spelling caused him much embarrassment over the years, and he had clearly come to the conclusion that while other educational deficiencies could always be overlooked or remedied, legible handwriting was an essential life skill that required extra attention.

Princess Elizabeth was cared for from birth by her mother's formidable but kind-hearted old nanny, Clara Knight, known to her adoring charges as 'Allah'

MARION CRAWFORD

The two princesses adored their Scottish governess, but their love quickly turned to disdain when she broke their trust

Born into an ordinary family in Gatehead, East Ayrshire in June 1909, Marion Crawford trained as a teacher after leaving school before studying to become a child psychologist, taking nannying jobs in order to supplement her income. When she joined the York household in the spring 1932, she was initially supposed to stay for just a month but was such a success that the position was made permanent and she remained with the family for 17 years. When she finally retired after Princess Elizabeth's marriage in November 1947, Crawford was given Nottingham Cottage at Kensington Palace as a home as a mark of the royal family's appreciation. Shortly afterwards, she was contacted by an American magazine, which offered to commission articles about the two princesses and their education, which, pressured by her new husband who was keen to capitalise on her connection with royalty, she agreed to do under her own name, despite the disapproval of her former employers. In 1950, the articles were followed by a book, *The Little Princesses*, which was an international bestseller but resulted in Crawford's complete ostracism by the royal family and the loss of her cottage. When she died in 1980 there was no acknowledgement from the royal family, and even many years later, the expression 'doing a Crawfie' was used by the family as code for anyone who betrayed their confidence.

However, his wife, Queen Mary, was rather more exacting and insisted that there should be particular emphasis on the teaching of geography and history, which she believed were essential topics for a potential future monarch. To assist in this worthy enterprise, she accompanied both of her granddaughters on regular visits to museums, art galleries and other sites of historical significance around London.

Although Crawfie did her best to give her charges as broad an education as possible, she was defeated by the fact that she was only able to teach Elizabeth for one and a half hours every morning, and even that precious time, which was not nearly enough for a bright and curious child of seven, was constantly interrupted. The rest of the day was taken up with meals, nap time and plenty of playing outside - which in the countryside involved riding lessons on her beloved Shetland pony, Peggy, a fourth birthday present from her doting grandfather, and one that ignited a lifelong passion for horses.

Although the Duke of York was second-in-line to the throne, he nonetheless hoped that his daughters would be free to enjoy their carefree, happy existence for several years to come - only to be disappointed when his father died in January 1936 and his brother succeeded the throne as Edward VIII. If the new king had also been happily married and father to a brood of promising children then the diffident Duke, who had absolutely no desire to one day become king - even if he was doubtless well aware that both of his parents had hoped that the crown would one day come to him - would have felt much more comfortable. However, his brother was still very much enjoying the hectic, louche existence of a wealthy bachelor prince. The only signs he showed of wanting to settle down were with Wallis Simpson, a divorcée of whom Parliament and the royal family thoroughly disapproved.

There was some talk at this time of sending Elizabeth to school, but her parents' determination to keep her at home and provide her with a happy childhood persevered and the lessons with Crawfie continued. As Elizabeth got older, more time was devoted to her lessons, and they covered an increasingly broad range of subjects, with poetry, literature and grammar being added to history and geography, although unfortunately

Although her education was rather patchy, Princess Elizabeth managed to develop a lifelong love of reading

Marion Crawford frequently took her charges on excursions in London, even on the Tube

Crawfie turned out to be unequal to the task of teaching maths at any advanced level.

Special tutors were brought in to teach the princesses dancing, music and French, although early French lessons did not always go well, with the small Elizabeth even upturning a pot of ink over own head during one particularly frustrating lesson. Such outbursts were rare though, as right from the start, Elizabeth was a conscientious, quiet and unusually well-behaved child - unlike her sister Margaret, who was wilful, naughty and high spirited. Music lessons were much more popular, with Margaret showing particular talent and becoming an exceptionally gifted pianist.

As the two sisters shared their lessons and never had any classmates or exams, they were relieved of the pressure of competing with other children of the same age. However, at the same time they had no real way to assess their progress, which left them feeling insecure about their intellectual abilities, despite the fact that their parents were so cheerfully unconcerned about the matter. The possibility of one day going to university was almost certainly never mentioned, even though at the time, increasing numbers of girls were going into higher education, with the result that much later in life Elizabeth would ruefully comment that she did not believe that she and her sister would have succeeded in getting places at university anyway.

Whatever hopes the Duke and Duchess of York might have had that their daughters would enjoy a normal, carefree existence were finally shattered towards the end of 1936 when Edward VIII signalled his intention to marry his mistress Wallis Simpson, who had recently divorced for the second time. The resulting crisis ended with the king's abdication in December, less than a year after he had succeeded to the throne, and the very unwilling succession of Elizabeth's father, who took the name George VI, while his eldest daughter became heir presumptive to the throne. The new royal family moved into Buckingham Palace within a few weeks, with Elizabeth and her

Princess Margaret joined her sister in the schoolroom at the age of seven, which she later felt was too late as she regretted not having more of an education

"THEY WERE RELIEVED OF THE PRESSURE OF COMPETING"

sister being assigned a very prettily decorated suite of rooms overlooking the Mall, with tall windows from which the two princesses could wistfully watch people go about their business down below.

Their lessons with Crawfie continued as normal but the new king's sense that he had been ill-

prepared for the daunting task ahead of him made him determined to ensure that his own heir should be better equipped when her time came. To this end, in 1938 he arranged that Elizabeth should travel to Windsor twice a week in order to take special private lessons in constitutional history with the Vice-Provost of Eton College,

PRINCESS ELIZABETH'S DAILY ROUTINE

The Duchess of York wanted her children's upbringing to be as happy and carefree as her own had been

The day would start early with breakfast in the nursery before the two princesses were taken downstairs to their parents' bedroom for 'high jinks' and private family time before the Duke and Duchess had to go about their day, which often took them out of the house until evening, and the girls went through to their schoolroom, which was next to their mother's bedroom. Lessons, which were frequently interrupted

by visits from dentists, doctors, dressmakers and photographers, would take place between 9.30 and 11, when they stopped for a snack and an hour of playing the garden, until midday when they had their nap, followed by an hour of Crawfie reading aloud, preferably from a book about animals. If their parents were at home, the princesses had lunch with them before spending the rest of the day playing. They

also had dancing and music lessons in the afternoon before they were taken downstairs to spend an hour with their mother before they had supper, followed by their daily bath, which the Duke and Duchess usually made a point of attending and which usually involved a lot of splashing and messing around. When the two little girls went to bed, they would call their goodnights to their parents from the top of the stairs.

Princess Elizabeth's daily routine involved more time playing outside than actual lessons

Princess Elizabeth adored her father's elder brother, the future Edward VIII, but their relationship became distant as she got older

Although Princess Elizabeth had a reputation of being a solemn, quiet and shy child, she was also cheerful and good natured

Princess Elizabeth learned to ride at an early age on a Shetland pony given to her by her grandfather George V. It was to be the first of many horses

Henry Marten. While Crawfie, who acted as chaperone, sat in the corner quietly reading, Marten taught his young pupil about history, government and the often confusing Constitution of the United Kingdom, the rules and legislation that determine the governance of the nation that she would one day reign over.

Although the subject matter was often extremely dry and she was occasionally daunted by the reading material, which included weighty tomes about English social history, law and politics, Elizabeth nonetheless enjoyed her sessions with Marten thanks to his engaging and gregarious manner. The chief cornerstone of the curriculum were the three volumes of Sir William Anson's *The Law and Custom of the Constitution*, which she dutifully read while taking notes and underlining the most significant passages, particularly those that related to her own future role. Gruelling and tedious though these studies must on occasion have been, they served her well as in later life; several of Elizabeth's prime ministers would be deeply impressed by her grasp of the Constitution.

Shortly after World War II broke out in 1939, the two princesses and their household moved to the relative safety of Windsor Castle, where they were to remain until the end of the war in 1945, often only seeing their parents at weekends. While at Windsor, their education continued as usual, with Elizabeth still having her lessons with Henry Marten, while the rest of the curriculum was, as always, covered by Crawfie, a French teacher, Mrs Montaudon-Smith, and dance and music tutors. Elizabeth supplemented all of this with her own private reading of books in the expansive royal library as well as avid readings of the weekly tabloid, *The Children's Newspaper*, subtitled 'The Story of the World Today for the Men and Women of Tomorrow', to which Crawfie had subscribed Elizabeth, hoping that it would increase her awareness and understanding of current affairs.

Fearing that her granddaughters were woefully ignorant about art, Queen Mary, who had become passionately interested in art history during her youthful sojourn in Florence, arranged for precious paintings from the Royal Collection to be placed on an easel in their schoolroom and did

her best to ensure that they were educated about the art treasures that hung on the walls of the royal palaces.

In 1942, Elizabeth's education was given a further veneer of sophistication when Vicomtesse Marie-Antoinette de Bellaigue joined the household in Windsor in order to give the two princesses lessons in French language and history, as well as an understanding of other nations and their customs. Under Madame de Bellaigue's directions, only French was spoken at mealtimes and the two girls quickly increased their fluency, while at the same time acquiring a little bit of French polish.

Elizabeth's education was formally considered to be at an end when she turned 18 in 1944, and although it had not been as rigorous as perhaps it should have been, especially when compared to that of past heirs to the throne, still her parents were very satisfied with how she had turned out. Any deficiencies were more than compensated for by her sensible, self-possessed manner, deep dedication to duty, and poise – essential qualities for a future queen.

Princess Elizabeth joins the ATS

As World War II raged on, Princess Elizabeth was determined to do her part for her country, begging her father to allow her to take part in the war effort. At the age of 18, her father finally relented and gave her permission to join the Auxiliary Territorial Service (ATS), a women's branch of the British Army. Here, Elizabeth trained as a mechanic and driver. She began as a lowly second subaltern, but by the end of the war the princess had reached the rank of junior commander.

— 1945 —

Prince Philip made a name for himself as a talented and heroic naval officer

THE PRINCE, THE NAZIS AND THE BROKEN HOME

Discover how the queen's "liege man of life and limb" overcame a tragic upbringing and emerged as a war hero and prince consort

Words by **Tom Garner**

Prince Philip, Duke of Edinburgh, was one of the most recognisable men in the world. As the husband of Queen Elizabeth II, he represented the British monarchy for well over 70 years. Before his death in April 2021, he was the longest-serving consort of a reigning British monarch. Along with the Queen, he had done much to represent the royal family as an unchanging institution in a world that changed almost beyond recognition since young Elizabeth succeeded to the throne in 1952. However, on Philip's part this security was in deep contrast to his early life, which was formed by war, neglect, tragedy and endurance. In many ways his long and successful marriage alongside his subsequent family compensated for the trials of his youth.

Philip was born on 10 June 1921 on the Greek island of Corfu at Mons Repos, the only son of Prince Andrew of Greece and Denmark and Princess Alice of Battenberg who already had four daughters: Cecilie, Sophie, Margarita and Theodora. Although typically seen as British today, Philip was born as Prince of Greece and Denmark. This dual title was reflected in his name. He was christened 'Philippos' but he belonged to the Danish-German House of Schleswig-Holstein-Sonderburg-Glücksburg. To add to the confusion, Philip was not a British subject at birth but did have family ties to England. His maternal grandfather, Prince Louis of Battenberg, was a naturalised British citizen who had adopted the surname of 'Mountbatten' during World War I. Philip was related to the British royal family through Queen Victoria, but he was also sixth in line to the Greek throne and his paternal uncle Constantine I was the ruling king. Nevertheless, his wider European connections would soon come in very handy for Philip as he was born during a turbulent time for Greece, and his stay in the country of his birth would not last long.

Philip's father was absent at his birth as he was away fighting in the Greek army during the Greco-Turkish War of 1919-22. During this conflict, Andrew was the commander of the Greek Second Army Corps, but he proved to be an ineffectual general. At the pivotal Battle of Sakarya on 19 September 1921, he refused to obey the orders of his superior officer and tried to work to his own battle plan. Unfortunately this lack of co-ordination and communication contributed to a battlefield stalemate, and subsequently the war was lost. Andrew was relieved of his command and a year later he was arrested as part of the 11 September 1922 Revolution. This was a revolt of the Greek armed forces against the government, who they held responsible for the Turkish victory. It led to the downfall of the Greek monarchy and the abdication of King Constantine. As the brother of Constantine and a disgraced army commander, Andrew was in deep trouble. He was accused of treason and initially sentenced to death. General Pangalos, the Greek minister of war, asked him, "How many children have you?" When Andrew replied, Pangalos reportedly said: "Poor things, what a pity they will soon be orphans".

When Princess Alice heard of Andrew's plight, she travelled to Athens to plead for his life but she was not permitted to see her husband, so she turned to her British relatives for help. King George V, who was possibly haunted by not allowing his cousin Tsar Nicholas II of Russia and his family to seek asylum in Britain during World War I, urged for a British intervention to evacuate the family.

Images © Toptoto

A Greek court banished Andrew from Greece for life and he was released in December 1922. He was lucky: six other senior members of the government were tried and executed. Soon afterwards a Royal Navy gunboat, HMS Calypso, evacuated the family from Corfu. Prince Philip, who was still a baby, was reputedly carried out to the ship in a makeshift cot made out of an orange box. For the infant, it was the start of decades of stateless wandering. From the moment Philip left Corfu on 3 December 1922 until he moved into Clarence House as Princess Elizabeth's husband in the late 1940s, he had no permanent home.

The family tried to settle in France at Saint-Cloud near Paris, where Andrew and Alice borrowed a house. From the start they lived in relative poverty. Alice was able to keep the family together on a limited allowance from her brother and Andrew was able to contribute a small legacy that he had inherited, but they mostly relied on borrowed funds and hand-me-downs. Relatives paid the children's school fees, with Philip's early education at the MacJannet American School in Paris. His life was confused - he was a Greek prince living in France but being educated in a British fashion. His stateless identity meant that he could formulate his own, which he later explained, "If anything I've thought of myself as Scandinavian, particularly Danish. We spoke English at home. The others learned Greek. I could understand a certain amount of it. But then the conversation would go into French. Then it went into German, because we had German cousins. If you couldn't think of a word in one language, you tended to go off in another."

In 1928 Philip went to Britain for the first time to attend Cheam School. He appears to have been a somewhat boisterous child that needed some discipline. Alice wrote to the school in 1929 asking his tutors to form a Cub Scouts company for her son with a hint of anxiety: "The training would have such an excellent influence on him... I should be infinitely grateful if you could manage it as soon as possible". By this stage Philip's family life was already beginning to collapse. Alice, who had been born deaf, was on the verge of a nervous breakdown. There has been much speculation as to what caused this. It has been variously attributed to the ordeal of the family's exile from Greece, the regular separations from her children as they attended different schools, a traumatic menopause, manic depression and even a possible religious crisis. It may have been one or a combination of these factors, but for whatever reason, Philip's mother was placed in a Swiss sanatorium in 1931.

At around the same time, Philip's sisters all married within nine months of each other between 1930-31 and moved away to settle in Germany. Prince Andrew, who had spent more and more time away from the Parisian family home, finally left altogether and moved to the south of France with a mistress. One relation said he was "a deeply unhappy man". Philip's sister Sophie said: "We all sort of disappeared and the house in Saint-Cloud was closed down."

"HE WAS A GREEK PRINCE LIVING IN FRANCE BEING EDUCATED IN A BRITISH FASHION"

Philip started his education at the MacJannet American School in Saint-Cloud, France. He is pictured with his schoolmates and is the second boy on the left

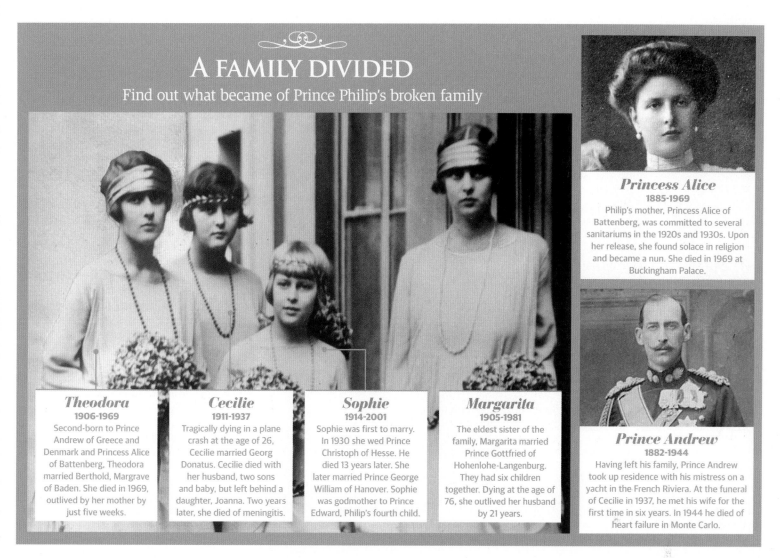

A FAMILY DIVIDED
Find out what became of Prince Philip's broken family

Princess Alice
1885-1969
Philip's mother, Princess Alice of Battenberg, was committed to several sanitariums in the 1920s and 1930s. Upon her release, she found solace in religion and became a nun. She died in 1969 at Buckingham Palace.

Prince Andrew
1882-1944
Having left his family, Prince Andrew took up residence with his mistress on a yacht in the French Riviera. At the funeral of Cecilie in 1937, he met his wife for the first time in six years. In 1944 he died of heart failure in Monte Carlo.

Theodora
1906-1969
Second-born to Prince Andrew of Greece and Denmark and Princess Alice of Battenberg, Theodora married Berthold, Margrave of Baden. She died in 1969, outlived by her mother by just five weeks.

Cecilie
1911-1937
Tragically dying in a plane crash at the age of 26, Cecilie married Georg Donatus. Cecilie died with her husband, two sons and baby, but left behind a daughter, Joanna. Two years later, she died of meningitis.

Sophie
1914-2001
Sophie was first to marry. In 1930 she wed Prince Christoph of Hesse. He died 13 years later. She later married Prince George William of Hanover. Sophie was godmother to Prince Edward, Philip's fourth child.

Margarita
1905-1981
The eldest sister of the family, Margarita married Prince Gottfried of Hohenlohe-Langenburg. They had six children together. Dying at the age of 76, she outlived her husband by 21 years.

Philip's parents had effectively relinquished responsibility for their son. This does not mean that they did not care for him - by all accounts he was much loved, but the circumstances of their own lives meant that they were unable to look after him properly. He was just ten years old and would receive no word from his mother between 1932 and 1937. When Philip was asked about this time years later his reply was stoic and pragmatic: "It's simply what happened. The family broke up. My mother was ill, my sisters were married, my father was in the south of France. I just had to get on with it. You do. One does."

In the aftermath of this disintegration, the British part of Philip's family took a large part of responsibility for his care. His maternal grandmother, Princess Victoria, sent him to live with his uncle George, Marquis of Milford Haven. He was Philip's guardian for the next seven years and became a surrogate father to him. Philip would become close friends with George's son David, who later was best man at his wedding to Princess Elizabeth. The two boys attended Cheam School, where Philip excelled at sport. The Marquis would often come to watch him and his son play in school matches. The Milford Havens gave Philip a sense of stability that was lacking

elsewhere but he remembered the upheaval as confusing. When he was later asked what language was spoken at home he replied, "What do you mean, at home?"

In 1933 Philip's second sister Theodora reappeared in his life and set him down the path towards a different education and introduced him to a significant mentor: Kurt Hahn. Theodora had married Berthold, Margrave of Baden, whose father had been Imperial Germany's last chancellor. Hahn had been the chancellor's personal secretary

Philip c.1935 at Gordonstoun dressed in costume for a school production of *Macbeth*

and knew the family, but he was also a committed educationalist. He was Jewish and a German patriot who had been involved in the 1919 Treaty of Versailles. He had been so upset at the Allied treatment of post-war Germany that he helped to coin the term, 'Kriegsschuldlüge' ('The lie of war guilt'). Ironically, the deeply anti-Semitic Nazi Party would use this message as an explosive slogan for revenge and rearmament, which was not Hahn's intention.

In 1920, he and the Baden family founded a school at Schloss Salem in Baden-Württemberg and it was here that Theodora sent Philip in autumn 1933. It was an anxious time to move to Germany as Adolf Hitler had recently come to power. He had only been in office for a few months, but it was enough to create political tensions, with Hahn himself being arrested for protesting against the Nazis. For Philip the move was bad timing and his brother-in-law admitted, "He wasn't really integrated into the community. He had little opportunity to make real friends, and he spoke very little German. He was really very isolated." In a sinister twist, the Nazis promoted the Hitler Youth Movement in the school, where participants would use the Nazi salute. Philip apparently laughed at this, as the salute was the

THE SISTERS WHO MARRIED NAZIS
Some of Philip's siblings had sinister connections to the Third Reich

Prince Philipp of Hesse was a member of the Nazi Party and the brother-in-law of Princess Sophie, Philip's sister

One sign of Philip's highly divided family was that some of his sisters had connections to the Nazi Party. All four had married into the German nobility: Margarita had married Gottfried, Prince of Hohenlohe-Langenburg; Theodora married Berthold, Margrave of Baden; Cecilie married Georg Donatus, Grand Duke of Hesse and Sophie married Prince Christoph of Hesse. It was traditional for European royal families to marry into foreign noble houses, but in the context of the 1930s, it was an out-of-date practice, particularly in the wake of World War I. Many surviving nobles tried to protect their positions by aligning with the radical social changes that were occurring throughout Europe. In the case of Germany, some sought to curry favour with the Nazis.

Sophie's husband Prince Christoph and his brother Philipp were great-grandsons of Queen Victoria and enthusiastic Nazis. Christoph was a prominent SS colonel who was attached to Himmler's personal staff and was the head of the intelligence service, the 'Forschungsamt', which spied on Nazi opponents under the command of Hermann Göring. Philipp had joined the Nazis in 1930 and was their governor in Hesse in 1933, and later served as a liaison between Hitler and Mussolini. Sophie and Christoph even named their eldest son Karl Adolf in Hitler's honour and Sophie said that Hitler was a "charming and seemingly modest man."

On 1 May 1937 Cecilie and her husband Georg, Duke of Hesse, also joined the Nazi Party, but they were killed in a plane crash. Their funerals became a Nazi pageant. Prince Philip walked alongside Prince Christoph who wore his SS uniform, and Philipp wore the brown shirt of the SA. There were also uniformed soldiers, and many onlookers gave the Hitler salute. Göring attended and there were messages of condolences from Hitler and Goebbels. When Prince Philip got married ten years later the British royal family excluded his surviving sisters and their husbands from attending the wedding, largely out of embarrassment and taking into consideration the anti-German feeling in Britain when the horrors of the Nazi regime had been realised.

same gesture that the boys at Schloss Salem used to indicate that they wanted to go to the toilet.

By 1934 Philip was sent back to Britain and was sent to a new school in Scotland that had been established by the now-exiled Hahn: Gordonstoun. The teaching methods developed by Hahn were radical and innovative. He believed that adolescents should be respected but were also susceptible to the corruptions of society. Hahn postulated that there were was a six-fold decay of civilisation, which he called 'The Six Declines of Modern Youth'. They were the decline of: fitness, initiative and enterprise, memory and imagination, skill and care, self-discipline, and compassion. Gordonstoun pupils were taught to counter these declines. For instance, they rose at 7am each day, donned shorts and ran barefoot for 300 yards to the washroom where they showered in cold water both in winter and summer. Philip was hardy, energetic and competitive, and flourished under this apparently tough regime. He excelled at hockey and sailing and in his last year became Head Boy. Hahn's philosophy had a great impact

on Philip and many years later he called on him to help found the Duke of Edinburgh's Award programme. Today the award scheme is active in 144 countries and recognises young people's achievements in self-improvement based on Hahn's Six Declines of Modern Youth. Such was Hahn's influence that when he died in 1974 Philip read the story of the Good Samaritan at his memorial service.

Despite Philip's achievements at Gordonstoun, he could not escape the fact that he was still very isolated. In the five years that he attended the school neither George Milford Haven nor Philip's other British guardian Lord Louis Mountbatten visited him. This is an extraordinary lapse for men who were technically responsible for him. During term-time there were long discussions about where Philip would go for his holidays. Towards the end of his time at Gordonstoun Philip was hit by a family tragedy. On 19 November 1937 his pregnant sister Cecilie was killed in plane crash in Belgium, along with her husband, two children and unborn child. She had been flying to England

to attend a wedding. Hahn conveyed the news to Philip, but the 16-year-old did not break down, which led his headmaster to recall, "His sorrow was that of a man." Nor did his fellow pupils remember Philip showing any signs of grief, with one remembering, "I suppose he just buried his feelings." Philip travelled alone to attend the funerals in Germany. It was a tragically strange occasion. Nazi officials surrounded the funeral parties but it was also the first time that Philip's parents had seen each other and their surviving children for years. They were the worst circumstances for a reunion, but Philip returned to Britain to fend for himself again.

The next year, 1938, brought new purpose to Philip's life in more ways than one. Under the advice of his father and Lord Mountbatten, Philip decided to join the Royal Navy and enrolled at the Britannia Royal Naval College at Dartmouth. He excelled at naval training and almost passed with top marks. His contemporary, Terence Lewin, who later became First Sea Lord said, "Prince Philip was a highly talented seaman. No doubt about it. If he hadn't become what he did, he would have been First Sea Lord and not me." This was an intense time to join the Navy as Britain was on the brink of war with Germany, but Philip's time at Dartmouth coincided with the first meeting of his future wife. In July 1939, Philip was put in charge of entertaining his distant cousins, 13-year-old Princess Elizabeth and her younger sister Margaret when they visited the college. They had met in 1934 and in 1937 at George VI's coronation but on this occasion Elizabeth fell for Philip. Over the next few years they would write letters to each other, but for the moment there were other priorities. There was a war to be fought.

Philip's war service began when he was posted to HMS Ramillies in Ceylon in January 1940. In the war's early days, he was posted far from action as Greece was not at war, and as a Greek prince the British did not want him to be killed on a Royal Navy ship. However, this changed when Italy invaded Greece and Philip became an active participant. At the Battle of Cape Matapan off the

The Battle of Cape Matapan, during which Philip was in charge of operating the ship's searchlight

During World War II, Philip was first officer on board HMS Whelp

"DURING TERM-TIME THERE WERE LONG DISCUSSIONS ABOUT WHERE PHILIP WOULD GO FOR HIS HOLIDAYS"

Greek coast in March 1941, Philip served as a midshipman on HMS Valiant where he was in charge of operating the ship's searchlight to pick out ships during the night. He recalled, "I reported that I had a target in sight and was ordered to 'open shutter'. The beam lit up a stationary cruiser and at this point all hell broke loose, as all our eight 15-inch guns, plus those of the flagship, plus HMS Barham's, started firing at the stationary cruiser, which disappeared in an explosion and a cloud of smoke. I was then ordered to 'train left' and lit up another Italian cruiser, which was given the same treatment". The ships identified by Philip were two of five Italian warships that were sunk by the British with the loss of 2,300 sailors. It was Italy's greatest naval defeat and Philip was mentioned in dispatches for his courage and awarded the Greek Cross of Valour.

The next year, at the age of 21, Philip was promoted to become one of the youngest first lieutenants in the Navy and in July 1943 he was once again in action, this time aboard HMS Wallace taking part in the Allied invasion of

Sicily. During a night attack, Wallace came under bombardment from a German plane. One yeoman sailor aboard the ship, Harry Hargreaves, recalled in a 2003 interview, "It was obvious that we were a target and they would not stop until we had suffered a fatal hit. It was like being blindfolded and trying to evade an enemy whose only problem was getting his aim right. There was no doubt in anyone's mind that a direct hit was inevitable." During a lull in the attack Philip acted quickly. "The first lieutenant (Philip) went into hurried conversation with the captain, and the next thing a wooden raft was being put together on deck." This raft was attached with smoke floats that created the illusion of debris ablaze on the water. The German plane was fooled into attacking the raft and the ship slipped away under the cover of darkness. Hargreaves praised Philip's initiative: "It had been marvellously quick thinking. Prince Philip saved our lives that night. I suppose there would have been a few survivors, but certainly the ship would have been sunk. He was always very

courageous and resourceful." Philip himself later talked about his plan in a BBC interview, describing it as "a frightfully good wheeze... we got away with it." Despite his nonchalance, even he managed to concede that "it was a very unpleasant sensation."

Philip ended his war aboard HMS Whelp, which was one of the ships that took part in the formal surrender of Japanese forces on 2 September 1945. He recalled, "Being in Tokyo Bay with the surrender ceremony taking place in the battle ship, which was what, 200 yards away and you could see what was going on with a pair of binoculars, it was a great relief". After the surrender his ship took on former prisoners of war and he was shocked by their appearance. "These people were naval people. They were emaciated... tears pouring down their cheeks, they just drank their tea, they couldn't really speak. It was a most extraordinary sensation."

Now that the war was over he expected to continue in his naval career, but fate had determined a different future for him...

The funeral of Princess Cecilie

On a flight from Frankfurt to London via Brussels, Philip's heavily pregnant sister, Princess Cecilie, went into labour with her fourth child. Already travelling in treacherous weather conditions, the pilot was forced to divert, but with Cecilie on the brink of giving birth, the pilot requested to land at Stene Airfield near Oostende in Belgium. Tragically the plane never made it, instead crashing into a factory chimney and killing all on board the flight, including all four crew, Cecilie, her husband, their two sons and newborn child, as well as Cecilie's mother-in-law. The family's funeral was held in Darmstadt, Germany, and was attended by Prince Philip, as well as Lord Louis Mountbatten. The pair were surrounded by the family's German relatives, including prominent Nazis, who saluted at the procession as it passed by.

— *November 1937* —

AN ENDURING LOVE

As Britain recovered from the horrors of World War II, it basked in the romantic love story of Princess Elizabeth and Prince Philip

Words by **Jessica Leggett**

For over 70 years, Queen Elizabeth and Prince Philip were the cornerstone of the modern British monarchy. The story of their relationship, from a young romance to their marriage and enduring devotion, endeared them to the public at a time when the majority of royals married for duty rather than for love. Their wedding came at a time when the people of Britain, weary from the war, craved a distraction, becoming one of the most celebrated events of the 20th century.

Princess Elizabeth was just eight years old when she first set eyes on her third cousin, Prince Philip, at the wedding of Princess Marina of Greece and Denmark to Prince George, Duke of Kent, in 1934. Five years later they would meet again, at the Royal Naval College in Dartmouth in July 1939. This time Elizabeth, now 13 years old, fell head over heels in love for Philip, who had turned into a handsome 18-year-old man.

The pair managed to spend a lot of time together that day, as Philip's uncle, Lord Louis Mountbatten, had arranged for his nephew to chaperone both the princess and her sister, Princess Margaret. After connecting at the college, Elizabeth and Philip agreed to exchange letters while they were apart and soon enough, the princess started to keep a framed photo of her beloved by her bed.

With the outbreak of World War II just months later, Elizabeth and Philip found themselves separated over the next six years, just like millions of other couples across the country. While Philip served in the British Royal Navy, the princess trained as a driver and mechanic, working for the Auxiliary Territorial Service in 1945. Elizabeth and Philip remained in contact during such harrowing times, with the latter even making a brief visit to Windsor to watch the princess perform in a pantomime with her sister.

When the war finally ended in 1945, there was a sigh of relief across Great Britain. Elizabeth and Philip were still in love and it became obvious to onlookers that their romance was indeed serious. Elizabeth's father, King George VI, invited Philip to Balmoral in 1946. It was during this visit that the prince took the plunge and asked Elizabeth to marry him, after seeking permission from her father. George consented, but on the condition that the engagement remain a secret until Elizabeth's 21st birthday in April 1947.

However, this was not just about giving Elizabeth time to consider her decision. Her father, along with the rest of the royal family, were concerned that Philip was not a suitable choice for the husband of the future queen. There were no advantages to be made from a marriage between the two - although Philip was a prince, he was practically penniless, and his family had been exiled from Greece after the abdication of his uncle, King Constantine I.

In addition to this, Elizabeth's family were well aware of the chaotic situation of Philip's parents. While Elizabeth had a close and loving upbringing, Philip was left alone to be raised in boarding schools. His mother, Princess Alice of Battenberg, was suffering with mental illness while his philandering father abandoned the family. With parents such as these, there were grave worries that Philip would not remain faithful to Elizabeth.

There were also concerns about Philip's connection to the Nazis in the wake of World War II. All four of his older sisters had married Nazis and when one of them, Cecilie, died in a plane crash in 1937, a young Philip was pictured at her funeral surrounded by the Nazis.

Of course, it was also impossible to forget the domineering presence of Philip's uncle and mentor, Lord Mountbatten. Ambitious and determined, it was no secret that Mountbatten was actively campaigning in favour of the relationship - to the point where Philip apparently admitted that his uncle was placing a lot of pressure on him to ask for Elizabeth's hand in marriage.

It is said that Elizabeth's mother, Queen Elizabeth, referred to her future son-in-law as "the Hun" and that even Winston Churchill was suspicious of the prince. Though Elizabeth was excited about her future with Philip, her family secretly hoped that within a year she would have changed her mind.

Elizabeth may have been a naturally shy woman, but her family wholly underestimated her determination to marry Philip. Adamant that she

The young couple looked very much
in love on their wedding day

would only marry him, King George and Queen Elizabeth were eventually forced to accept their daughter's relationship.

In the lead up to the announcement of their engagement, Prince Philip renounced his Greek and Danish titles and became a naturalised British citizen, subsequently adopting the last name 'Mountbatten', which was from his mother's British family. Philip also converted to Anglicanism in preparation for his marriage to the future Supreme Governor of the Church of England.

On the 9 July 1947, less than three months after Elizabeth's 21st birthday, the royal engagement was announced to the world. While the couple basked in the happiness, it seemed that it was not only Elizabeth's family that had reservations about the match. A newspaper poll that was held soon after the announcement indicated that 40% of the public were against the marriage - unsurprising, as Philip was considered too 'German' following the conclusion of the war.

Yet when it became clear that the couple were marrying for love rather than duty, those who initially opposed the marriage soon warmed up to it. After all, a glamorous royal wedding was a welcome distraction for many in Great Britain and a great way to boost morale in the country.

With the wedding date set for the 20 November and with just four months to plan the event, preparations quickly got under way. It wasn't until mid-August that the design for Elizabeth's wedding dress, by Sir Norman Hartnell, was approved, giving the renowned designer less than three months to create his masterpiece.

Wedding fever was running high throughout the nation (and worldwide), but with post-war austerity still in place, Elizabeth had to save up her clothing ration coupons in order to pay for the material of her dress - in total it took 3,000 coupons. To help her, hundreds of brides-to-be sent their own coupons to the princess so that she could use them. Although this was a very endearing gesture, the coupons all had to be returned to their owners as it would have been illegal for Elizabeth to use them because they belonged to others.

The government did provide Elizabeth with 200 extra coupons to pay for her wedding dress while Philip, never one for extravagance and spending, planned to wear his naval uniform for the big day. The couple would marry at London's Westminster Abbey, where Elizabeth's parents, King George and Queen Elizabeth, had married just over 24 years earlier, making the princess the tenth member of the royal family to be in this spectacular setting.

It was decided that Elizabeth would have eight bridesmaids including her sister HRH Princess Margaret, her cousin HRH Princess Alexandra of Kent, Lady Caroline Montagu-Douglas-Scott, Lady Mary Cambridge, The Hon. Pamela Mountbatten, The Hon. Margaret Elphinstone, Lady Elizabeth Lambart and Diana Bowes-Lyon.

As for Philip's best man, he chose David Mountbatten, the Marquess of Milford Haven, while Prince William of Gloucester and Prince Michael of

Elizabeth walking up the aisle at Westminster Abbey with her father

"WEDDING FEVER WAS RUNNING HIGH THROUGHOUT THE NATION"

Kent would serve as page boys. In total, 2,000 guests were to be invited to the wedding ceremony, many of whom were heads of state, such as Princess Juliana and Prince Bernhard of the Netherlands and the king of Iraq. Notably absent would be Philip's sisters as well as Elizabeth's uncle, the Duke of Windsor, who had caused a constitutional crisis just a decade earlier by abdicating the throne.

King George VI and his wife held a grand ball at Buckingham Palace just two days before the

Elizabeth and Philip are pictured here after announcing their engagement

wedding to celebrate their daughter's upcoming marriage. The usually reserved King George even led a conga line through all of the state rooms in the palace. On the morning of the wedding, Prince Philip was made Duke of Edinburgh, Earl of Merioneth and Baron Greenwich. The day before, King George had bestowed the title of 'His Royal Highness' on Philip, which meant that for a few hours, the prince had the unusual title of His Royal Highness Sir Philip Mountbatten.

Philip had spent the night before his wedding at Kensington Palace, and with hordes of photographers outside in the bitter cold waiting for him to emerge, Prince Philip arranged tea and coffee for them. Meanwhile, Elizabeth was getting ready at Buckingham Palace, even applying her own makeup for the wedding.

Just like any wedding day, not everything went as smoothly as the princess would have liked. Her delicate bridal bouquet, delivered that morning and made of white orchids and a sprig of myrtle, had gone missing. The myrtle had come from Osborne House, where Queen Victoria had planted a cutting that had been given to her by Prince Albert's grandmother. As panic set in, it turned out that a footman had placed the bride's bouquet in a cool room to keep it fresh and prevent it from wilting.

The bouquet was not the only unfortunate mishap of the morning. Elizabeth's mother had lent her the Queen Mary Fringe Tiara to be her something borrowed on her special day. As it was

DRESSING FOR THE DATE

Elizabeth's wedding dress was a sumptuous but modest creation perfect for the post-war years

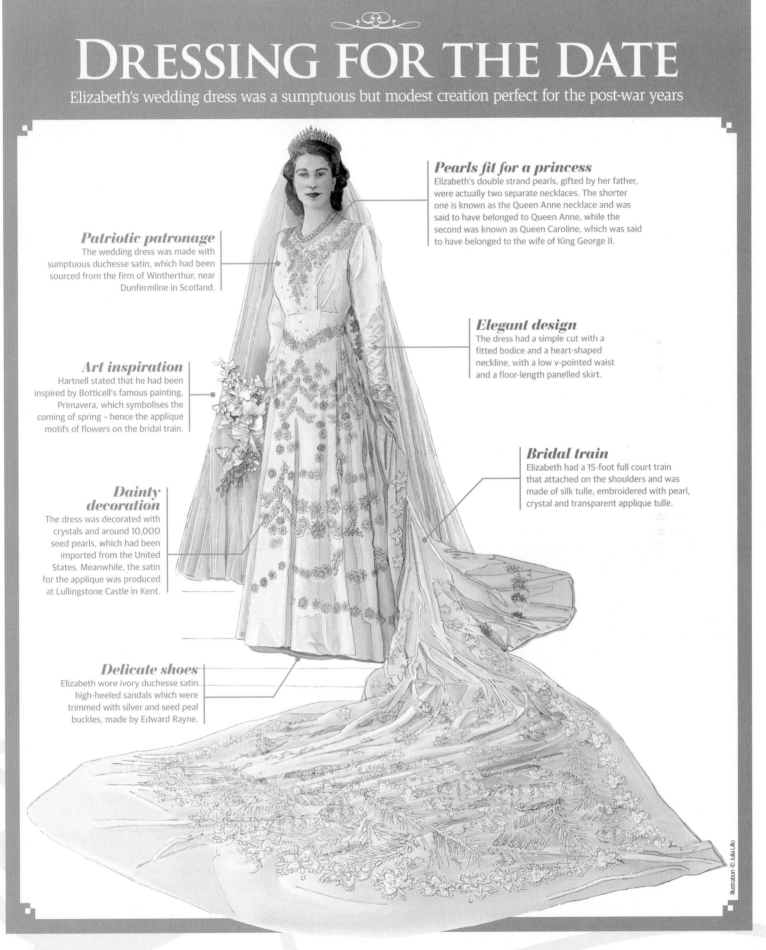

Pearls fit for a princess
Elizabeth's double strand pearls, gifted by her father, were actually two separate necklaces. The shorter one is known as the Queen Anne necklace and was said to have belonged to Queen Anne, while the second was known as Queen Caroline, which was said to have belonged to the wife of King George II.

Patriotic patronage
The wedding dress was made with sumptuous duchesse satin, which had been sourced from the firm of Wintherthur, near Dunfermline in Scotland.

Elegant design
The dress had a simple cut with a fitted bodice and a heart-shaped neckline, with a low v-pointed waist and a floor-length panelled skirt.

Art inspiration
Hartnell stated that he had been inspired by Botticell's famous painting, Primavera, which symbolises the coming of spring – hence the applique motifs of flowers on the bridal train.

Bridal train
Elizabeth had a 15-foot full court train that attached on the shoulders and was made of silk tulle, embroidered with pearl, crystal and transparent applique tulle.

Dainty decoration
The dress was decorated with crystals and around 10,000 seed pearls, which had been imported from the United States. Meanwhile, the satin for the applique was produced at Lullingstone Castle in Kent.

Delicate shoes
Elizabeth wore ivory duchesse satin high-heeled sandals which were trimmed with silver and seed peal buckles, made by Edward Rayne.

Illustration © Julia Lillo

A ROYAL HONEYMOON

How Elizabeth and Philip spent their first few days as newlyweds

As the bride emerged from Buckingham Palace to embark on her honeymoon, she wore a dress and velvet coat with a bonnet trimmed with ostrich feathers, designed by Norman Hartnell, in an appropriate shade of love-in-the-mist blue. The king and queen, along with Princess Alice, came out to wave the couple off.

Elizabeth and Philip were driven to Waterloo station in an open landau carriage so that the waiting crowds could see them – to ward off the cold, there were hot-water bottles of the floor of the carriage, along with Elizabeth's beloved corgi, Susan. As the carriage departed, the newlyweds were showered with rose petals rather than traditional confetti.

Elizabeth and Philip travelled to Broadlands in Hampshire, the home of Philip's uncle Earl Mountbatten, where they spent the first half of their honeymoon in an 18th century lodge – in 2007, the couple re-created their iconic honeymoon photo at Broadlands. Afterwards, they moved on to Birkhall Lodge, which was part of the Balmoral estate, to see out the rest of their honeymoon.

While they were away, Elizabeth and Philip released a statement expressing the gratitude they felt for all the well-wishes they had received. The princess also kept in touch with her family and lovingly informed her mother that Philip was "an angel".

Elizabeth and Philip pictured in Malta following their marriage

The beaming bride after her fairytale wedding

"ELIZABETH'S DRESS WAS EXHIBITED AT ST JAMES'S PALACE BEFORE EMBARKING ON A TOUR"

being placed on her head, disaster struck as the diamond tiara suddenly snapped. Standing by in case of an emergency was the court jeweller, who was rushed to his workroom by a police escort. Elizabeth waited anxiously and her mother quickly reassured her that the tiara would be fixed in time – and it was. To top off the issues for the bride-to-be, the necklace that she supposed to wear, a double strand of pearls gifted to her by her parents, had been put on display at St James's Palace. To get them in time, Elizabeth's private secretary raced to the palace, borrowing the car of King Haakon VII of Norway to make it in time.

Despite the bumps along the way, the princess and the prince were finally ready for their wedding,

which was due to start at 11.30am. The royal parties arrived at the abbey in large carriage processions, past the thousands of onlookers who had lined the streets to get a glimpse of the royal bride. Queen Elizabeth and Princess Margaret were the first to arrive, followed by Dowager Queen Mary.

Prince Philip left Kensington Palace accompanied by his best man and entered the abbey through a door near Poet's Corner. Meanwhile, Elizabeth made her way inside the decadent Irish State Coach, with her father by her side, escorted by the Household Cavalry. As the coach approached Westminster Abbey, the bells of St Margaret's Church rang out to announce the blushing bride's arrival. Outside, the princess was joined by her large bridal party. As the radiant bride made her way inside Westminster Abbey, she must have been acutely aware that the entire ceremony was being

recorded and broadcast by BBC Radio to 200 million people. Waiting at the High Altar was the Archbishop of Canterbury, Geoffrey Fisher, who officiated the wedding.

At the High Altar there were large vases filled with white lilies, roses, pink carnations, camellia foliage, variegated ivy and chrysanthemums. Clement Attlee, the prime minister at the time, and other politicians were sat in the choir stalls with King George VI and Queen Elizabeth sat in the south side of the Sanctuary.

The organist and master of the choristers at the abbey, William Neil McKie, was the director for the music. The ceremony began with a fanfare specifically composed for the wedding by Arnold Bax, while McKie also composed a motet for the wedding, "We wait for thy loving kindness, O God." Sir Edward Cuthbert Bairstow sung a rendition of

Crowds lined the streets just to get a glimpse of the bride

The magnificent wedding cake

Psalm 67 and in total, there were 91 singers at the wedding with the combined choirs of Westminster Abbey, the Chapel Royal and St George's Chapel in Windsor.

The couple exchanged their vows. Elizabeth's wedding ring was made from a nugget of Welsh gold, which came from the Clogau St David's mine, near Dolgellau. The gold had been given as a gift to Queen Elizabeth to make her wedding ring and, eventually, the wedding rings of Princess Margaret, Princess Anne and Princess Diana were all made with it.

After the couple finished their vows, they moved into St Edward's Chapel behind the altar in order to sign their marriage register, accompanied by immediate members of their family. Once the register had been signed, the couple walked out of the Abbey to Felix Mendelssohn's classic *Wedding March*.

Following the wedding ceremony, the newlyweds left Westminster Abbey to return to Buckingham Palace. The wedding breakfast was held in the Ball-Supper Room at lunchtime, with a menu of "filet de sole Mountbatten, perdreau en casserole, and bombe glacée Princess Elizabeth". Princess Elizabeth, taking into account the post-war rationing of food, only had 150 guests attending the wedding breakfast.

While the guests tucked into their food, they enjoyed the music provided by the string band of the Grenadier Guards. The delicate wedding favours were made from individual posies of myrtle and white heather, from the royal estate of Balmoral in Scotland.

The stunning wedding cake was made by McVitie and Price. It was nine-feet tall, separated into four tiers, and was made from ingredients that had been sent from all over the world. Even the sugar that was used had been provided by the Girl Guides in Australia, and as the result the cake was nicknamed 'The 10,000 Mile Cake'. The cake was decorated with the arms of the bride and groom's families, monograms of the bride and groom, sugar-iced figures of their favourite activities and also decorations of regimental and naval badges. Elizabeth and Philip cut the cake with the sword that had been gifted to the groom by his new father-in-law. Although this was the official wedding cake, the couple had received 11 wedding cakes in total. In fact, they received over 2,500 gifts and 10,000 telegrams of congratulations from well-wishers - Gandhi had even sent a piece of cotton lace that he spun himself, embroidered with the words 'Jai Hind' or 'Victory for India' in English.

To greet those who had gathered on the Mall, Elizabeth and Philip made their way onto the balcony and waved to the adoring crowds. The next day, Elizabeth's wedding bouquet was sent back to Westminster Abbey to be laid on the Tomb of the Unknown Warrior, a royal tradition that had been started by her own mother when she had married in the wake of World War I.

The wedding fever that had consumed Britain did not end once the special day was over. Elizabeth's dress was exhibited at St James's Palace before embarking on a tour across the country, giving the public an opportunity to view it up close. The palace also exhibited all of the gifts that the couple had received for the public to enjoy, while cinemas held screenings of the wedding ceremony across the country.

A couple of years into their marriage, Philip relinquished his beloved and promising naval career to support his wife, as she assumed more responsibility in the wake of her father's declining health, proving to all that he would be a reliable consort to Elizabeth.

In 2007, Elizabeth became the first British monarch to celebrate a diamond wedding anniversary. When Prince Philip passed away at the age of 99 in April 2021, 74 years had passed since their magical wedding that lifted the spirit of the nation. Over those decades, Elizabeth and Philip proved that love can, indeed, last a lifetime.

Images ©Getty

Philip, the wartime hero

After finishing his formal education at Gordonstoun, Philip joined the Royal Navy, studying at the Royal Naval College in Dartmouth where he graduated as his course's best cadet in 1940. Despite his Greek heritage and German connections, Philip served for Britain during WWII. Proving his worth as a brave and loyal sailor, he quickly worked his way through the ranks, achieving the commission of first lieutenant by the time he was 21 years of age. Famously, in July 1943, while second-in-command of HMS Wallace, he saved his ship from bombing by creating a diversion that enabled it to slip away unnoticed. After marrying Princess Elizabeth in 1947, Philip continued to serve in the Royal Navy, but was forced to sacrifice his esteemed career when George VI died in 1952.

— *1939-1945* —

THE DEATH OF GEORGE VI

He may have steered his country through the chaos of World War II, but the stress took its toll on Britain's beloved monarch

Words by **Jessica Leggett**

Members of the public lined the street to pay their respects to their king

It was 6 February 1952. The king's valet, James McDonald, was up bright and early to attend to His Majesty. As usual, he started to prepare a bath for the king, knowing that the running water would be enough to wake him. But as the bath continued to fill up and the telltale signs of the king's footsteps could not be heard, McDonald's heart sank. Entering the king's bedroom to see a lifeless body, he rushed to get the doctor, who confirmed his fears - King George had died in his sleep.

Plagued with health problems and a heavy smoker for most of his life, George had been in decline for quite some time. His arteries had hardened and he had to give up a number of public appearances due to severe pain in his right leg and foot, caused by Buerger's disease. In fact, George almost lost his right leg due to an arterial blockage and had to be given a lumbar sympathectomy in March 1949. George's poor health, as well as his smoking habit, had been exacerbated due to the stress of World War II and the post-war years. He had led his country admirably and along with his family had become a symbol of hope during the dark times of war. But it was a lot to deal with, particularly for a naturally anxious man who had reluctantly agreed to bear the crown.

Following the issues with his right leg, George's tour to Australia and New Zealand had to be postponed. It was decided that the tour should be rearranged so that George's eldest daughter and heir, Princess Elizabeth, could go instead with her husband Prince Philip. As the king's health increasingly declined, Elizabeth began to take on a lot more responsibility to support her father, who she absolutely adored.

However, the worst was yet to come. In May 1951, the king was able to open the Festival of Britain, but it was painfully clear that he was unwell. He underwent X-rays that revealed a shadow had developed on his left lung. Hoping to avoid alarming the king, his doctors told him that he was suffering with a mild form of pneumonia, which could be treated with penicillin injections.

The next month, Princess Elizabeth attended the Trooping of the Colour on behalf of her father while he tried to recover. Yet over the coming months it became evident the king was suffering from something worse than a bout of pneumonia. After more tests it was confirmed that a malignant tumour had been found in George's left lung. It was recommended to the king that he undergo an operation to have the affected lung completely removed. George felt uneasy about going under the knife, but his doctors assured him that it was the best possible treatment. To prevent him and the rest of his family from becoming even more anxious, they claimed that 'structural changes' necessitated the removal of the lung, rather than admitting that it was, in fact, cancer.

The streets of London were filled with people wishing to pay their respects to the king

King George pictured at London Airport a week before his untimely death at Sandringham

For the operation, a makeshift operating theatre was constructed on the first floor of Buckingham Palace, complete with an operating table, lighting and other surgical equipment. It was the best way to keep the king's condition under wraps and to ensure he had privacy during the operation.

The operation to remove the lung was conducted on the 23 September 1951, led by Clement Price Thomas, who was ultimately made a Knight Commander of the Royal Victoria Order for his service to the king. George had been injected with anaesthetic inside his own room before he was wheeled to the theatre. While his left lung was successfully removed, the doctors' worst fears were confirmed during the operation - the cancer had also spread to the king's right lung. At best, George had a year to live.

Although the prognosis was not good, George's doctors resisted telling him the devastating news that he was suffering with lung cancer. The only person who appeared to work it out was the king's close friend and former prime minister Winston Churchill, who deduced the gravity of George's illness after discussing the matter with his own doctor. In the meantime, George concentrated on his recovery, attempting to get out of bed for a few minutes each day to improve his poor circulation.

By October the king was still unwell. Unable to leave his bed to attend the Privy Council, a small delegation of the councillors were forced to gather around his bedroom door in order to conduct business. As for Princess Elizabeth, she journeyed to Canada with Prince Philip for a month-long tour, which had already been postponed because of her

"AFTER MORE TESTS IT WAS CONFIRMED THAT A MALIGNANT TUMOUR HAD BEEN FOUND"

The Queen Mother, the new Queen Elizabeth II, and Princess Margaret in mourning

George restored public faith in the monarchy after his brother sparked the abdication crisis in 1936

Pictured in 1948, the toll of WWII and his smoking habit had physically aged the king beyond his years

Princess Elizabeth started taking on more and more responsibility as her father's health began to falter

A MOVING TRIBUTE

Churchill remembered his close friend King George in one of the most emotional speeches of his life

Originally disliking one another, the friendship between King George and Winston Churchill had developed during the turbulent years of World War II. They famously met in private once a week in order to discuss any developments in the war while enjoying a spot of lunch together.

Churchill had known for some time that George was dying. The day after George's death, he travelled to London Airport to greet his new sovereign, Queen Elizabeth, as she returned from Kenya. On the way there he dictated a speech, which would be broadcast that afternoon, in honour of his friend and king. According to one of his secretaries, the iron-willed Churchill was "in a flood of tears".

Churchill's emotional eulogy has gone down in history as one of his most eloquent speeches. In one particular passage, Churchill spoke of the king's illness and declared, "The last few months of King George's life, with all the pain and physical stresses that he endured – his life hanging by a thread from day to day, and he all the time cheerful and undaunted, stricken in body but quite undisturbed and even unaffected in spirit – these had made a profound and an enduring impression and should be a help to all."

His words, a tribute to his dear friend, perfectly summed up the difficulties that King George had bravely faced in his final years. With an uneasy start, Churchill would soon develop a close relationship with Elizabeth, mentoring her through the first three years of her reign until his retirement in 1955.

The king and Winston Churchill became firm allies after the latter's election as prime minister

father's illness. With concern rising about the king's condition, Elizabeth's private secretary, Martin Charteris, carried with him a draft Accession Declaration and a message to the Houses of Parliament, just in case George died while they were away.

The king's spirits were lifted when Churchill was elected as prime minister once again on 25 October, and he seemed to be improving. By 14 November he was well enough to attend Prince Charles's third birthday, and that December George was able to pre-record his annual Christmas broadcast for that year. He then travelled to Sandringham for Christmas with his family, even managing to enjoy a few rounds of shooting across his estate.

As the end of January approached, Princess Elizabeth and Prince Philip were preparing to head out on a tour of Australia and New Zealand via Kenya. The tour had long been in the works and the original plan had been for George and his wife Queen Elizabeth to go, but the king was still not well enough to travel. Even so, nothing would stop George from seeing his daughter off at London Airport on 31 January, despite medical advice that he should not go.

George's appearance at the airport was the last time he would be seen by the public. He spent his final days at Sandringham, and on 5 February, the day before his death, George enjoyed what would be his last day of shooting. His footman, Daniel Long, had taken a warm cup of cocoa up to the king at 11pm, not realising that he would be the last one to see George alive. At 7.30am the next morning, George was found dead in his bed after suffering a coronary thrombosis (a blood clot to the heart) in his sleep. He was only 56.

Just over an hour since George had been declared dead, the codeword for his passing, 'Hyde Park Corner', was triggered by his principal private secretary, Sir Alan Lascelles. When Churchill was informed of the 'bad news' he blustered, "Bad news? The worst!" As the seriousness of the king's health had not been made known to the public his death came as a shock to many.

Sadly, one of the last people to discover the news of George's passing was Princess Elizabeth, who had spent the night at the remote Treetops Hotel in Kenya observing wildlife. Upon receiving the news she hastily returned home with the rest of the royal party - at 25 years old she was now the new monarch of the United Kingdom.

As news of the king's death swept the country, Union Jacks were flown at half-mast, shops and factories were closed for the day and members of the public began to arrive outside Buckingham Palace to mourn. George's coffin was kept at St Mary Magdalene Church, Sandringham, for two days before it travelled to London via train and subsequently moved to Westminster Hall to lie in state from 11 February, where more than 300,000 people arrived to get one last glimpse of their highly respected king.

George's funeral was held on 15 February at St George's Chapel at Windsor Castle, with his body interred in the Royal Vault. The Government sent a wreath - made from white and lilac carnations - in the shape of the George Cross, the award founded by George, with the phrase 'For Valour' written on a card by Churchill. In 1969, George's body was transferred from the Royal Vault to the King George VI Memorial Chapel, which was also located inside St George's Chapel.

After spending just over 15 years on the throne, George had restored faith in the monarchy after the disastrous abdication of his brother, King Edward VIII. Remarkably, the funeral of George's youngest daughter, Princess Margaret, was held exactly 50 years later on 15 February, 2002. The royal family would suffer another tragedy when George's wife, remembered now as the Queen Mother, passed away just seven weeks later. The Queen Mother, along with Margaret's ashes, were interred in the Memorial Chapel, reunited with their father, husband and Britain's endearing king.

Elizabeth arrives at Sagana Lodge

On the first leg of their Commonwealth Tour in 1952, Princess Elizabeth and Philip visited Kenya, where they stayed in the beautiful Sagana Lodge. The royal couple were returning to the lodge from the Treetops Hotel on 6 February when word arrived that George VI had passed away in his sleep. The new queen immediately returned to the UK. In a poignant line in the Treetops visitors' book, Jim Corbett, a celebrated hunter and her guardian at the hotel, wrote: "For the first time in the history of the world, a young girl claimed into a tree one day a Princess and after having what she described as her most thrilling experience she climbed down from the tree next day a Queen – God bless her."

— *February 1952* —

Princess Margaret as
photographed by her husband
Antony Armstrong-Jones in 1959

PRINCESS MARGARET'S FORBIDDEN LOVER

Beautiful, wealthy and spoiled, Princess Margaret wanted for nothing – so why was her love for a dashing war hero doomed to fail?

Words by **Catherine Curzon**

Once upon a time, there lived a princess who had almost everything that a girl could dream of. Beautiful, privileged and the envy of everyone who knew her, all that was missing to complete the happy picture was a real-life prince charming. And who better to fulfil the role than a hero of the Royal Air Force who was as handsome as she was lovely; a man with a chestful of medals and the trust of the king himself? For the princess and her Spitfire ace this should have been a fairy tale come true, yet the tangled, tragic love life of the late Princess Margaret never truly found its happy ending.

Her Royal Highness Princess Margaret Rose was born in 1930 to Albert and Elizabeth, the quietly domesticated Duke and Duchess of York who shunned the social whirlwind she would later plunge into. Margaret's elder sister was a young lady named Elizabeth, better known to us today as Queen Elizabeth II. To their parents, however, Margaret and Elizabeth were simply Margot and Lilibet, the daughters they adored. During Princess Margaret's idyllic childhood, there was no suggestion that she would one day be the daughter of a king, let alone the sister of the longest-reigning monarch in British history. Fate, however, has a habit of moving in the most mysterious ways and, in 1936, romance brought scandal to the House of Windsor.

Less than 11 months after he ascended the throne, King Edward VIII abdicated. Passionately in love with American divorcée Wallis Simpson, Edward was faced with a choice between romance and duty. The king famously chose to follow his heart, turning his back on royal privilege to be with the woman he adored. When Margaret faced the same decision years later, her conclusion was not so romantic.

As Edward left England to start his new life, the world changed forever for those he left behind. Margaret's father was a timid, shy, man who famously struggled to control a debilitating stammer and certainly had no ambitions to rule as king. Yet he knew that he could not refuse the role that duty now demanded him to take and, in December 1936, was enthroned as King George VI.

At just six years old, Margaret Rose was no longer simply the daughter of a shy, unassuming duke. Now she was second-in-line to the throne itself and the quiet life she enjoyed at 145 Piccadilly was over. The royal family took up residence in Buckingham Palace, yet Elizabeth and Margaret, though suddenly catapulted to the forefront of public attention, found their lives little changed as the days went by.

The new king and queen did all they could to ensure that their daughters enjoyed as normal a childhood as possible. They attended Brownies and visited family, remaining safely out of the public eye. The girls were educated as young ladies and spoiled rotten by their doting parents, especially the king. While young Elizabeth was prepared for the role that one day awaited her, Margaret had no such burden to bear and the world lay at her feet.

Images © Getty

The Princess photographed by Victor Blackman as she arrives back on English soil after travelling in Canada

As Margaret blossomed into a young woman, she began to indulge her love of glamour and the finer things in life. Slender, graceful and as beautiful as any fairy-tale princess, she had a passion for fashion and whether sparkling on the red carpet or indulging in her beloved philanthropic events, she delighted in being the centre of attention.

Margaret also had a keen intelligence and a sharp, biting wit; people longed to be part of her circle, and she was soon at the beating heart of society. Although she was not yet an adult, it was clear that Margaret would one day be a most eligible princess indeed.

When Princess Margaret was 17, she accompanied her parents on an official visit to South Africa; it was to be a fateful trip. For the duration of the visit, Margaret was chaperoned by Group Captain Peter Townsend, a 33-year-old former RAF officer who was one of the king's most trusted equerries. Townsend was a bona fide war hero, a character cut from the mould of a matinee idol. Handsome, assured and urbane, he had won the Distinguished Flying Cross in 1940 for his heroic deeds. Townsend flew in the Battle of Britain, even surviving a ditch into the ocean. His career was glittering, and even wounds sustained in combat couldn't stop him - just

weeks after losing a big toe to the surgeon's knife, the Group Captain was back in action, flying Spitfires into battle.

At the end of World War II, Townsend retired from the Royal Air Force and joined the Windsor household as an equerry of King George VI. He became a valued and trusted member of the king's intimate circle and would later be appointed comptroller of the Queen Mother's household, a mark of his high status. Perhaps it should come as no surprise that the beautiful young princess and the handsome, experienced RAF officer fell madly in love. There could not be a happily ever after for the couple though, because Townsend wasn't just dashing, brave and celebrated - he was also already married.

While Elizabeth married Prince Philip and settled into the role of wife, mother and queen-in-waiting, Margaret's own life was a whirlwind of social engagements, excitement and laughter. She had no shortage of admirers and even found time in her packed calendar to perform royal duties and support a range of charities. What really caught the eye of the press and public, however, was how much she liked to socialise, and she was always the belle of the ball.

The world dealt Princess Margaret a shattering blow in 1952 when, on a bleak February day, lung cancer claimed the life of the 56-year-old king. George and Margaret had been devoted to one another, with the monarch always indulging his youngest child's wishes and, some argued, helping to nurture that spoiled, entitled little rich girl that some claimed she had become.

Now, with the death of her father, Margaret was left bereft. The woman who had been alive with happiness and joy sank deeper and deeper into depression and despair, utterly overwhelmed by her grief. Without her father's influence and support she was suddenly cut adrift. All that had seemed so set in her world had now been turned on its head.

With Elizabeth now queen, Margaret was also deprived of the good counsel of her sister and as the new monarch and her family moved into Buckingham Palace, Princess Margaret and her mother left for Clarence House. With them they took their new comptroller, a certain Group Captain Peter Townsend. Amid the emotional tumult, he was more than happy to lend Margaret a strong shoulder to cry on.

In fact, the change of employment was not the only turning point in Townsend's life. Like Margaret, he too was caught in a period of emotional turmoil thanks to his ongoing divorce. However, the story behind the breakdown of the Townsend's marriage hints at scandal beneath the official explanation.

In 1941, Townsend met Rosemary Pawle, and she was bowled over by the dashing young man. After just two weeks together the couple were married and over the next four years, two sons were born to the Townsends. Perhaps unsurprisingly given their fortnight of courtship, the marriage didn't work out in the long term, but the official reasons for the split remain tantalisingly vague. Called away from home first by his military duties and then by his services to the king, Townsend was increasingly absent from his family. Tired of being married to a man she rarely saw, Rosemary sought comfort elsewhere and began an affair with John de László, a dalliance that finally resulted in the couple's divorce in 1952.

Or so the papers believed. Rosemary and Townsend, however, remained tight-lipped even as the decades passed. No matter how much money the papers offered the former husband and wife to

A photograph of Margaret taken in the 1950s

"THEY ATTENDED BROWNIES AND VISITED FAMILY, REMAINING SAFELY OUT OF THE PUBLIC EYE"

spill the beans, both understandably refused to offer any behind-the-scenes gossip about the breakdown of their marriage.

In fact, when George VI died in 1952, Princess Margaret had never felt so alone, so utterly despairing, and in her grief she sought some measure of comfort from those she trusted. Not for her were the platitudes of her socialite friends

nor the society gents who filled her dance cards, it was to Peter Townsend that she turned. Though there is no reliable evidence that the couple became lovers in 1952, it doesn't take too much of a leap of faith to suppose that - even if they weren't sexually intimate - their relationship had certainly moved beyond chaperone and chaperoned. By the time Townsend filed for

GROUP CAPTAIN PETER TOWNSEND

Meet the war hero who swept Margaret clean off her feet

Group Captain Peter Townsend was born in 1914 and before he turned 20, was soaring through the clouds with the Royal Air Force. It was the start of a career that would be lauded as high-flying in more ways than one.

Townsend's celebrated World War II record is a roll call of victories, near misses and heroic escapes, including one ditch in the ocean and even an amputated toe! When his injury kept him from flying he retained control of his squadron and was back in the air before a month had passed. Within six short months, Townsend had earned the Distinguished Flying Cross and Bar in recognition of his efforts.

When the war ended, the celebrated Spitfire ace was welcomed into the royal household as a trusted equerry to the king. By the time Townsend met Princess Margaret in 1947, he had already been married for over five years and was the father of two children. His marriage ended in 1952, conspicuously just before his romance with Margaret and his proposal to her became public knowledge.

In the years following the end of their affair, Peter Townsend was posted to Brussels as air attaché at the British Embassy. It was here in Belgium that he fell in love with his secretary, Marie-Luce Jamagne, a woman who would later be noted for her striking resemblance to his royal former lover.

Townsend's 1959 marriage to Marie-Luce was a happy one. The couple had children and were together until his death more than 40 years later. Later in life, Townsend became a writer specialising in military history, as well as penning a biography of George VI. In his own autobiography he shared precious few details of the tumultuous romance he had enjoyed with the princess, preferring to keep those particular secrets to himself. Group Captain Peter Townsend died of stomach cancer at his home in France in 1995. He was 80 years old.

divorce that November, he and Margaret were certainly closer than they had ever been before, and the stage was set for scandal and heartbreak.

In 1953, Queen Elizabeth II was still settling into her reign and preparing for a grand and glittering coronation. The last thing she needed was a domestic drama, yet when Peter Townsend asked Princess Margaret to marry him, drama was just what the new queen was about to get.

Of course, the excited young princess was thrilled to receive Townsend's proposal and hoped to accept him, but she could not do so without the approval of her sister. Although it might seem strange that she had to request her sibling's permission, the Georgians can be thanked for that particular loophole. The Royal Marriages Act, enshrined in law in 1772, set down the stringent rules under which members of the royal family could marry, its intention being to protect the integrity of the royal household. Central to its power was the clause that all members of the family must secure the official consent of the reigning monarch before they were permitted to marry their betrothed.

For those over 25 there was a very small get-out clause, however. In this case, so long as Parliament didn't refuse the marriage, then the wedding could take place after one year, whether or not the monarch had given consent.

So Margaret found her future decided by a rule that was almost 200 years old, and in Townsend she had found a far from perfect candidate. Not only was he much older than her, but he was also divorced. With the fate of Edward VIII and Wallis Simpson fresh in her mind, Margaret must have guessed what the answer would be even before she sought permission. Even worse, the Church of England didn't recognise the marriages of those who were divorced as legitimate unions, rendering the couple's position even more precarious.

In fact, Queen Elizabeth II didn't immediately refuse the request but instead asked her sister to wait a little longer before she made a decision. This would give everyone a chance to cool off, let Elizabeth adjust to her new role and also mean that Margaret was 25, the age at which she could marry without her sibling's permission. However, the news of the couple's relationship leaked out following the Queen's coronation, an occasion at which Margaret and Townsend appeared to have eyes for nobody but each other. In a moment of unguarded domestic intimacy unthinkable for the brittle, headscarf-clad woman that Princess Margaret would become, she reached out to flick a piece of lint from Townsend's jacket. The tabloids loved it and so did the British people, who wanted to see the nation's sweetheart happy.

With public opinion rallying behind Margaret, the queen moved Townsend out of Clarence House and back to Buckingham Palace, yet Parliament had even more dramatic schemes in mind. The government flatly refused to sanction the marriage unless Margaret agreed to renounce her royal rights and privileges and gave up her

Margaret and Peter Townsend photographed during the Royal Tour of South Africa, 1947

"MARGARET MUST HAVE GUESSED WHAT THE ANSWER WOULD BE EVEN BEFORE SHE SOUGHT PERMISSION"

right to the throne. Should she agree to abandon her place in the line of succession, then Margaret would be free to marry her love in a civil ceremony. Should she wish to retain her rights of succession, even though she was highly unlikely ever to be queen, then there was no way that Margaret could marry Townsend.

A committed Christian, the choice was a stark one for Princess Margaret and she knew that her decision might have ramifications for the whole nation. She was separated from Townsend physically when the government had him posted to Brussels and, after long, agonising battles with her conscience, she made her decision.

A letter uncovered in 2009 from Princess Margaret to the prime minister, Anthony Eden,

Dated 18 October 1955, the *Daily Mirror* preoccupied its front page with the love life of Margaret

reveals that she had entertained other doubts about the marriage and was struggling with her decision. In the crucible of the public eye and press attention, the young woman was determined to make the right choice, and make it alone, regardless of what anyone else might tell her. When she did make her statement renouncing Townsend, however, it was one that he had written for her, carefully setting down the words in a neat pencil script.

Citing the Church's stance on the marital status of divorcées, as well as her duty to her sister's subjects, Margaret took to the airwaves to inform the nation that she could not marry Peter Townsend. "Mindful of the Church's teachings that Christian marriage is indissoluble, and conscious of my duty to the Commonwealth," she declared, the couple went their separate ways. Yet were these noble words heartfelt, or merely intended to cover up a more cynical motive? It has since been speculated that Margaret's decision was driven not by Christian faith, but by her own love of pomp and ceremony, and the fact that she simply would not give up her royal lifestyle and privileges for love. Where her uncle had followed his heart, Margaret had, according to some, followed her ego.

As the years passed, Princess Margaret and Peter Townsend were never close again. Courted by eligible suitors from across the world, she never entertained another proposal until, in 1959, Townsend told Margaret that he was to remarry. The very next day, the princess accepted an offer of marriage from photographer Antony Armstrong-Jones, later Lord Snowdon. Once again Margaret had chosen a far from ideal candidate, but at least this time he was not a divorced father of two.

As a social and fashion icon, Margaret's life was never far from the headlines or from the whispered gossip of society salons. Her name was linked with lovers as diverse as Warren Beatty, David Niven and Robin Douglas-Home – who took his own life when their romance ended. As she and Snowdon lived increasingly separate lives, Margaret began an affair with Roddy Llewellyn

that reached heights of emotion that drove the princess to attempt suicide. Around 17 years her junior, Llewellyn was a tabloid dream and just weeks after his romance with Margaret was splashed across the front page of the press, she and Snowdon publicly announced the end of their marriage. In 1978, the photographer and the princess were divorced.

Princess Margaret never remarried. Peter Townsend died in 1995 and she passed away in 2002. As the years sped by, she became a symbol of snobbish grandeur, the hedonistic sister who grew bitter in the shadow of her sibling, yet once she had been the focus of goodwill from a public who believed she deserved to be happy. Later, her unheard-of decision to divorce Snowdon catapulted the issue of royal marriage into the

public eye. Her experience blazed a trail for those who would follow, ensuring that divorce became accepted in the royal household. No longer were members of the House of Windsor expected to suffer in silence and in the years that followed, several of her nieces and nephews followed her into the divorce courts.

Although Townsend and Margaret occasionally exchanged letters, they did not meet again for almost four decades. Quite by chance, the former lovers encountered one another at a Kensington Palace luncheon. Time had healed whatever wounds their separation had wrought and the two made a beeline for each other. Here, they spent the afternoon together, chatting like old friends and catching up on all that had happened to each other over the years.

"IN A MOMENT OF DOMESTIC INTIMACY, SHE REACHED OUT TO FLICK LINT FROM TOWNSEND'S JACKET"

Peter Townsend photographed with his wife, Marie-Luce Jamagne, whose resemblance to Princess Margaret was uncanny

51 · H. SOUTHEY

Princess Margaret is photographed at 1am leaving the home Mr and Mrs Wills at 49 Kinnerton Street, where she'd dined with Townsend. He was seen leaving moments later, returning to his own flat

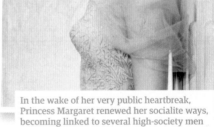

In the wake of her very public heartbreak, Princess Margaret renewed her socialite ways, becoming linked to several high-society men

Whether Princess Margaret's decision to reject the proposal of Peter Townsend and turn her back on love in favour of title was inspired by snobbish self-importance or religious and dutiful adherence to protocol, we will never truly know. Townsend, however, had his suspicions and wrote in his autobiography that Margaret had not been prepared to give up "her position, her prestige, her privy purse." His words are gently written, but particularly scathing to interpret. Famed for her love of partying, her scandalous liaisons and her altogether bohemian ways, whether Princess Margaret would have been suited to life as the wife of a war hero is equally mysterious. She lived life to the full yet surely, sometimes, Princess Margaret Rose must have looked back on the road that she chose not to take and wonder wistfully 'what if'.

THE LETTER THAT WAS NEVER PUBLISHED

In anticipation of accepting Townsend's proposal, a letter was drafted and ready to go

On Friday 2 January 2004, the secrecy surrounding a series of classified documents finally expired. Among the files held at the National Archives Office in London was correspondence between Buckingham Palace and the Prime Minister's Office regarding Princess Margaret's very public love life.

Filed with the official letters was one very startling piece of sentimental history: a drafted letter written by Princess Margaret, which acknowledged her intention to marry Peter Townsend, and agreeing to relinquish her claim to the throne.

Ultimately, however, Princess Margaret decided to follow her head and not her heart, and instead issued an announcement on the 31 October 1955 declaring that she would not go ahead with the marriage to Townsend. Her drafted letter of acceptance was never published.

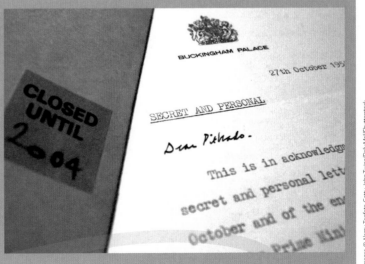

CLOSED UNTIL 2004

BUCKINGHAM PALACE

27th October 195

SECRET AND PERSONAL

Dear P'thado.

This is in acknowledg

secret and personal lett

October and of the en

Prime Min

Townsend's new family

In the wake of his very public break-up with Princess Margaret, Peter Townsend spent several years seemingly single until his shock engagement announcement to Marie-Luce Jamagne in 1959. The couple went on to have three children together; two daughters and a son. The couple remained in the public eye after their wedding. In 1963, Marie-Luce had an uncredited role in the film *Merci, Natercia*, while Peter wrote several books and articles, as well as contributing to the film *Battle of Britain* as one of several military advisers.

—— *1962* ——

A spectacular view from the very top of Westminster Abbey down to the coronation theatre, where the Queen is about to be crowned

GLORIANA

The coronation of Elizabeth II took nearly 18 months to plan and was heralded as the beginning of a bright and promising new age for a country still beleaguered by post-war austerity

Words by **Melanie Clegg**

"What is the finest sight in the world?" Horace Walpole wrote to a friend after witnessing the crowning of Elizabeth II's ancestor George III in 1761. "A coronation". The hallowed walls of Westminster Abbey had witnessed six coronations, all of them with more than their fair share of drama, since that of George III in the middle of the 18th century. Although each successive monarch imposed their own personality and wishes on the event, the solemn, ancient ceremony always remained essentially the same, employing regalia and following rituals that had been in use for several centuries, such as the order of service laid out in the *Liber Regalis*, a precious 14th-century book that had most likely been written at the time of the crowning of Anne of Bohemia, consort of Richard III and then used for all subsequent coronations.

Nonetheless, when Princess Elizabeth, eldest daughter of George VI, inherited the throne in February 1952, there were expectations that her coronation ceremony would be particularly impressive, with innovative touches that reflected the technological advances that had been made since her father's coronation, 16 years earlier in 1937. In the intervening years, Britain had been ravaged by war and although eight years had passed since the celebrations of VE Day, the nation had not yet fully recovered from its gruelling

ordeal. Much of London had been rebuilt, but many parts of the capital still looked sadly dilapidated and were riddled with ugly bomb sites, which served as a stark reminder of the horrors of the Blitz. Although food supplies were gradually improving, the economy had not yet recovered and some aspects of rationing would remain in force until the summer of 1954.

Now that the euphoria and relief that followed the end of the war had died away, the general mood across the nation was bleakly despondent as people struggled to rebuild not just their homes but also their lives, while at the same time dealing with the effects of the post-war economic austerity. The death of the universally beloved George VI at the beginning of 1952 only served to increase the gloom that pervaded the country, where the late king was respected and loved for his steadfast leadership during the war, and over 300,000 people patiently queued for hours in order to pay their respects when his coffin lay in state in Westminster Hall.

Preparations for the new monarch's coronation began almost immediately after the death of her father, although as was traditional, it was expected that a decent mourning period of around a year and a half would elapse before the actual crowning took place. Although the death of the King George VI had been greeted with genuine sorrow, the accession of his daughter was regarded as a sign of better times to come, perhaps even a

'New Elizabethan Age' to rival that presided over by her namesake Elizabeth I who, coincidentally, had also been just 25 years old when she succeeded to the throne. Princess Margaret later described it as "like a phoenix time. Everything was being raised from the ashes".

To underline what was anticipated to be the beginning of a new golden age for Britain and its people, it was decided to hold the coronation the following summer. This was in the hope of ensuring that the big day, which was chosen from a Met Office list predicting the most sunny days of the year, would have glorious sunshine - only for it to pour with rain and be one of the coldest June days on record.

Although the weather, as always, proved to be beyond human control, great efforts were made to ensure that every other aspect of the day went as smoothly as possible. The Coronation Commission, who were tasked with organising the event, met for the first time four months after George VI's death, with the Duke of Edinburgh acting as chairman at the Queen's request. According to tradition, unlike their female counterparts, male consorts of female rulers were not crowned alongside them during the coronation ceremony, which meant that Philip would not be consort. Conscious that her proud and energetic husband was already feeling rather ignored and sidelined by the establishment that surrounded her, the new Queen was naturally

A Buckingham Palace footman waits to help the Queen and Duke of Edinburgh down from the Gold State Coach

" AROUND 277 MILLION PEOPLE WATCHED THE CORONATION AROUND THE WORLD "

keen to ensure that he was as involved as possible in the preparations for the ceremony. Traditionally, the organisation of the coronation was presided over by the Duke of Norfolk in his heredity capacity of Earl Marshal, which involved being in charge of all major royal ceremonies. Although the current duke retained full control of the arrangements, he would this time be liaising with the Duke of Edinburgh, who was already brimming with ideas and would prove to be an invaluable asset over the coming months – although one of his first suggestions – that the ceremony be televised – immediately brought him into conflict with his wife and several others on the committee.

In 1952, just 14 per cent of UK households had a television set, with even more having access to one, and the number was set to rise even more over the next few years. For the Duke of Edinburgh, keen to modernise and invigorate the institution of royalty, televising the coronation ceremony was a perfect opportunity to reinforce the relationship between crown and populace, by ensuring that his wife's subjects could feel like actual participants in the ceremony. However, if he had expected the Queen to be in full agreement with his suggestion then he was about

to be proved wrong. She strongly opposed the notion, feeling like it would be undignified for the sacred moment of crowning to be broadcast into people's sitting rooms, where they might not be behaving in a properly respectful manner. She was also aware that previous coronations had been riddled with mistakes, such as the famous incident when Queen Victoria's coronation ring was forced on to her finger despite being far too small for her, and had no wish for any gaffes to be witnessed by millions of viewers. She was backed by several members of cabinet and the Archbishop of Canterbury, who considered television to be "potentially one of the greatest dangers of the world".

At first they prevailed but the announcement in October 1952 that the ceremony would not be televised was greeted by such universal disappointment and dismay – the populace having

become used to royal events being televised – that they were eventually forced to backtrack. However, at the Queen's request, there were to be no close-up shots of her face and certain parts of the ceremony, such as the anointing and Communion, would not be broadcast as they were considered to be too sacred.

On the day, over 27 million people watched the coronation in the UK, with an estimated 277 million watching worldwide thanks to sterling efforts by television companies who arranged that films of the event should be flown overseas as quickly and efficiently as possible, meaning that viewers in some countries were able to watch the coverage on the same day.

The unprecedented presence of television cameras presented new problems for the committees organising the event, particularly those tasked with liaising with Westminster

Cecil Beaton's photographs of the Queen on her coronation day remain among some of the most iconic royal portraits in history

PRACTICE MAKES PERFECT

Determined that the Queen's big day should go without a hitch, the organisers insisted that there should be several rehearsals beforehand

In the weeks before the big day, several rehearsals were carried out in Westminster Abbey in order to ensure that the coronation ceremony would be as perfect as possible. However, the Queen preferred to rehearse in private in the ballroom of Buckingham Palace and also spent several hours a day wearing the heavy St Edward's Crown, which weighed nearly five pounds, while she went about her business. As the big day drew nearer, she quietly attended two of the dress rehearsals at Westminster Abbey, where the Duchess of Norfolk acted as her stand in. The rehearsals not only gave everyone an opportunity to practise but also pinpointed any issues that might cause problems on the day, particularly with the live broadcast of the ceremony. An MP who attended one of the rehearsals reported that in his opinion, the Queen's maids of honour looked too pale under artificial light and recommended that they apply make up in order to appear more tanned so they wouldn't look washed out on television. On another occasion, the Earl Marshal decided that all of the page boys looked too scruffy and ordered them to get haircuts, threatening to report them to their headmasters if they did not comply. All of this preparation was felt to be worth it in the end though as the coronation itself passed almost without hitch – although there was an awkward moment at the end of the royal and state processions when the doors opened and everyone stood up, expecting the Queen, only for a group of cleaners to make an appearance and start vacuuming the carpet ready for the main procession, much to the audience's amusement and the horror of the Archbishop of Canterbury.

Queen Elizabeth spent hours practising for her coronation as the robes and regalia were so heavy and difficult to manage

Abbey, where the utmost care had to be taken to ensure that the building was returned to the exact same state once the event was at an end. As part of the preparation, a large-scale model of the Abbey was created to help officials plan the logistics of the day, which would involve increasing the normal seating capacity of the building from 2,100 to 7,500 and make enough space for what would ultimately amount to 8,251 guests, as well as adding a temporary annexe and all the facilities, such as 52 drinking water fountains, lavatories and even ten small sick bays, which were necessary to ensure the comfort and safety of such an enormous gathering of people.

The abbey closed to the public on the first day of 1953, which gave the organisers five months to prepare the interior - a mammoth task that involved covering the floor with a temporary wooden floor, boarding over the monuments and then erecting scaffolding to build the many tiers of seating for the guests. Meanwhile the annexe was being erected, it having been decided that it should look modern rather than being constructed in a pseudo-gothic style that had been favoured in the past.

The coronation regalia, including the crown itself, were to be housed in the annexe until they were required and it was also fitted with robing rooms for the Queen and the Duke of Edinburgh and a kitchen that served refreshments to the royal family, attendants and numerous peers taking place in the processions. Although the committees were keen for the ceremony and its setting to be as splendid as possible, they were always acutely aware that many of the population were still suffering the effects of post-war austerity and that they needed to be sensitive to this fact while making their arrangements. In the end, the coronation was estimated to cost £1.57 million (around £40 million in 2019), which included the cost not just of the abbey's decoration, but also the processions to and from Buckingham Palace, stands for the spectators and street decorations.

While the Coronation Committee was working on the details of the service and complicated logistics of what would be one of the grandest royal ceremonies of the century, the Queen's favourite designer, Norman Hartnell, who had also designed her wedding dress in 1947, was working on her coronation gown. Following Queen Elizabeth's direction, Hartnell submitted eight different designs in varying degrees of ornateness until she finally selected a white satin gown richly embroidered with the floral symbols of Great

Britain and the Commonwealth, which were picked out in gold bullion thread and embellished with crystals and pearls. The gown took eight months to make and towards the end required three dressmakers and six embroiderers from the Royal School of Needlework to work around the clock to ensure that it would be ready in time for the big day. As a final touch, Hartnell incorporated a tiny four-leaf clover on the left-hand side of the skirt, where the Queen's hand would brush against it during the ceremony.

Along with the coronation gown, Hartnell also designed the colobium sindonis, the traditional plain white linen dress that the Queen donned after her anointing along with the cloth of gold supertunica. As well as Elizabeth's dresses, Hartnell also designed the satin gowns worn by her six maids of honour, who complained that they were extremely itchy as they had been left unlined, as well as a new robe for peeresses, who were required to wear a special crimson velvet robe trimmed with miniver to the ceremony. As the basic design for this garment had changed very little over the years, many women were able to wear robes that had been passed down through their families, but for those who were not fortunate to have one stored in the attic, buying a new one was an expensive necessity. Beneath their robes, the peeresses wore ball gowns and their most splendid jewels, although, clearly at least one of the peeresses attending the event was rather careless with her belongings as after the coronation was over, the cleaning staff found a discarded diamond necklace, which remained unclaimed for six weeks.

On 24 March 1953, Queen Elizabeth's formidable grandmother Queen Mary died in her sleep at the age of 85. There were just ten weeks to go before the coronation but any fears that it might have to be postponed were allayed when it was revealed that the late queen had stipulated in her will that it should go ahead as planned. The presence of her eldest son, the former Edward VIII, now Duke of Windsor, who had been visiting her in London at the time of her death, also caused some

Queen Elizabeth arrives at Westminster Abbey for her coronation, carrying a bouquet of flowers like a bride to symbolise her wedding to her country

"THE GOWN TOOK EIGHT MONTHS TO MAKE"

embarrassment to the royal family as, at the request of Queen Elizabeth who did not want him there, he had not been invited to the coronation. When Edward asked Winston Churchill to intervene, the prime minister took the Queen's side and informed the former king that it would be inappropriate for him to attend and then advised him to issue a face-saving press release

stating that he did not plan to be there, which the duke duly did, although with very poor grace. When Edward was not invited to his niece Elizabeth's wedding in 1947, his sister, Princess Mary, had also refused to attend to show solidarity with her snubbed brother – this time, however, she accepted her invitation to the coronation and the rest of the royal family also closed ranks in order

THE OFFICIAL PHOTOGRAPHS

Cecil Beaton's photographs of the Queen in her coronation regalia are among the most iconic and familiar royal portraits in history

Although the Duke of Edinburgh had expressed a wish that his friend, the society photographer Baron, who had taken his wedding photos, should be awarded the honour of taking the official photographs to mark the Queen's coronation, he was swiftly overruled by his wife and her mother, both of whom insisted that the job had to go to Cecil Beaton. Excited and thrilled to be asked, Beaton

began to prepare several months in advance by ordering two enormous backdrops, one painted with the interior of Westminster Abbey's beautiful Lady Chapel, for the Queen to pose in front of in the temporary studio set up in Buckingham Palace's Green Drawing Room. Aware that the Queen was exhausted after her long day, Beaton tried to work as quickly as possible even though the lighting

was less than ideal and the Duke of Edinburgh, still irked not to have got his own way about the photographer, was bossing him about. At the end of the brief session, Beaton wasn't even sure that any of the photographs were useable and so was delighted and relieved when he discovered how well they had turned out despite the intense pressure that he had been under while taking them.

The Duke of Edinburgh's behaviour exasperated Cecil Beaton while he was taking the official photographs

An official photograph of the Queen with her Mistress of the Robes and six maids of honour, who carried her train throughout the ceremony - a task that they found rather arduous as it was extremely heavy

CORONATION OF HER MAJESTY
QUEEN ELIZABETH II

By Command of The Queen
the Earl Marshal is directed to invite

to be present at the Abbey Church of Westminster on the 2nd day of June 1953

Norfolk.
Earl Marshal

An official invitation to the Queen's coronation, which was attended by 8,251 guests. Prince Charles received his own specially hand-painted invitation to his mother's big day

to show support to the young ruler. Elizabeth also had huge amounts of support in the Houses of Parliament, where the coronation was universally regarded as a new, regenerative start for the nation, even if some Labour MPs expressed concern about the cost of such an event at a time of austerity. The press were also enthusiastic, particularly overseas, where Queen Elizabeth was a very popular figure thanks to her youth, prettiness and royal glamour. In the run-up to the coronation and immediately afterwards, newspapers and magazines were filled with stories and articles about the Queen and her family as the pageant and glitter of the coronation, which had cost nearly £2 million, dispelled the last lingering impression that Britain, once one of the most powerful nations on Earth, was still languishing in a battered and beleaguered state almost a decade after the end of the war.

Coronation day started at dawn for the stewards tasked with preparing Westminster Abbey for the event and they were amused to find Matins, one of the abbey's cats, fast asleep on the Coronation Chair when they started to arrive. Elsewhere, the guests were rising early in order to get ready as they were expected to be in their seats by 8.30am. They had a long wait until the service began at

11.15am, with many smuggling in books, sandwiches, flasks of coffee and miniature bottles of gin, whisky and brandy to sustain them as they waited - one of the archbishops astounded a group of page boys by revealing that he had sandwiches concealed beneath his mitre. Many of the guests had with them that morning's newspapers, which proudly proclaimed that a British team of climbers led by Edmund Hillary had become the first men to successfully reach the summit of Everest.

When the Queen, who was wearing the George IV State Diadem, arrived at 11am, the Earl Marshal, armed with a clipboard, quickly organised her procession, which comprised 250 people who all needed to be marshalled into the correct places. "Ready, girls?" the Queen asked her maids of honour as the organ began to play and they started to make their way towards the altar, where in her nervousness, she accidentally forgot to make the traditional curtsey. The rest of the ceremony passed without any serious mistakes and the guests watched in awe as the Queen was formally presented to the throng by the Archbishop of Canterbury, receiving their shouts of acclaim with a curtsey. During the early planning stage of the coronation, there had been

some arguments about whether it was appropriate for the Queen to curtsey to her people - perhaps surprisingly, her husband had expressed the opinion that it was undignified for her to do so, while the Queen insisted that it was the right thing to do and, in the end, got her way. After this, she then gravely took an oath upon the Bible to govern her people fairly, mercifully and without prejudice, after which she donned a plain white tunic and then, beneath a gold canopy held over her by four Knights of the Garter, was anointed with sweetly scented holy oil made to a formula first created for the coronation of Charles II in 1661. After the anointing, the Queen knelt for a blessing and then donned the white robe and supertunica in order to be invested with the royal regalia and then, finally, crowned, with the front of St Edward's Crown helpfully marked with a tiny gold star on the velvet so that the Archbishop of Canterbury would know which way to place it.

The royal family and their attendants gathered on the balcony of Buckingham Palace to watch a special RAF flypast over London. This was probably the highlight of the day for the royal children

"THE CROWD STRETCHED ALL ALONG THE MALL AS FAR AS TRAFALGAR SQUARE"

As soon as the crown was in place, the entire congregation shouted "God save the Queen," and the peers and peeresses donned their own coronets. The anointed and crowned young Queen then proceeded to the throne, where she received the homage of her peers and leading churchmen, with the Archbishop of Canterbury, as senior prelate of the Church of England, leading the way, followed by the Duke of Edinburgh, who happily knelt before his wife and declared himself to be her "liege man of life and limb" before kissing her cheek. At one point during the three-hour ceremony, the Queen glanced up at the balcony where her four-year-old son Prince Charles was watching, flanked by his grandmother and aunt, Princess Margaret, and smiled at him.

The ceremony ended with the new Queen and her husband taking Communion before retreating into the chapel behind the altar screen in order to exchange the heavy St Edward's Crown for the less cumbersome Imperial Crown, don her new purple Robe of State and have a nip of brandy from a flask produced by one of the archbishops, before she solemnly led the procession back out of the Abbey and into the annexe, where they were to rest and have lunch, which had the newly invented coronation chicken as one of the courses.

After lunch, which the Queen barely touched, the royal couple clambered back into the Gold State Coach for the return journey along a five-mile route to Buckingham Palace. The procession, which was two miles long and incorporated 46 bands and 16,000 participants, as well as 30,000 members of the armed forces, took an hour and 40 minutes. The cumbersome royal carriage moved slowly enough for most of the many thousands who had patiently lined the route since early in the morning - many of them spending the previous night sleeping on the pavement to ensure that they got a good spot - to get a good glimpse of the Queen, who gamely smiled and waved for the entire trip.

Upon her return to the palace, the Queen was immediately whisked off to have the official photographs taken by Cecil Beaton, who felt under pressure to produce his best work in the least possible time. After this, the royal family made their first appearance of the day on the balcony of Buckingham Palace, where they waved at an enormous, cheering crowd, which stretched all along the Mall as far as Trafalgar Square. There had been some who had questioned whether such an ancient and religious rite and associated celebration was appropriate for the modern age, but they were effectively silenced by the enthusiasm with which the coronation was received by the press and, most importantly, the populace. Even the Soviet Ambassador, Yakov Malik, representing a communist state, was noted to appear very moved by the service with, as one witness later recalled, "a look on his face of a kind of sadness that this was something outside himself". For most, the coronation had transformed the country, increased their prestige overseas and, most importantly, given them hope for a brighter future with the second Queen Elizabeth standing proudly at the helm.

CORONATION GARB

Discover the ornate outfit that Elizabeth II wore to her ceremony

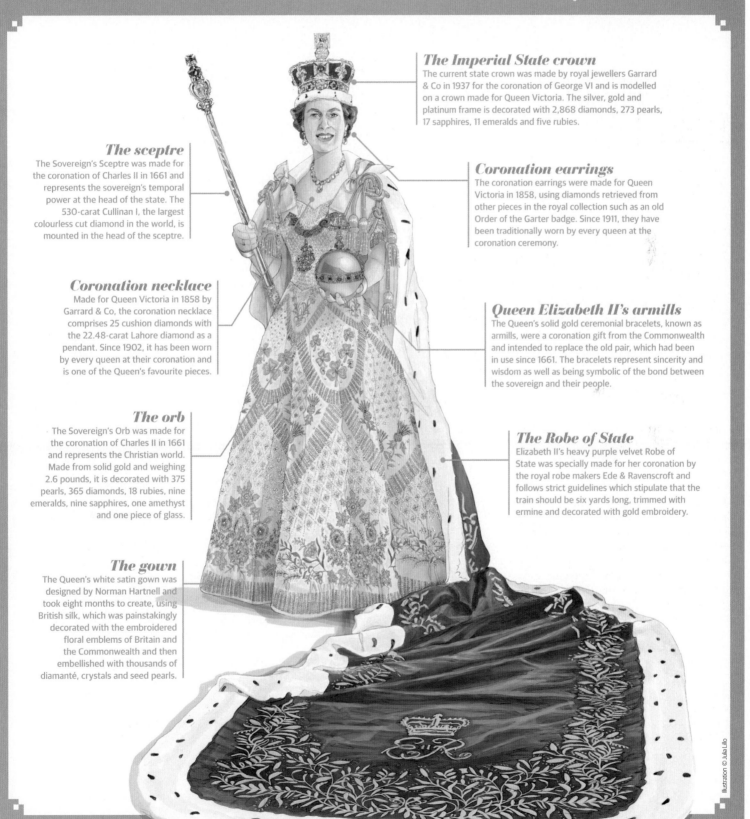

The Imperial State crown

The current state crown was made by royal jewellers Garrard & Co in 1937 for the coronation of George VI and is modelled on a crown made for Queen Victoria. The silver, gold and platinum frame is decorated with 2,868 diamonds, 273 pearls, 17 sapphires, 11 emeralds and five rubies.

The sceptre

The Sovereign's Sceptre was made for the coronation of Charles II in 1661 and represents the sovereign's temporal power at the head of the state. The 530-carat Cullinan I, the largest colourless cut diamond in the world, is mounted in the head of the sceptre.

Coronation earrings

The coronation earrings were made for Queen Victoria in 1858, using diamonds retrieved from other pieces in the royal collection such as an old Order of the Garter badge. Since 1911, they have been traditionally worn by every queen at the coronation ceremony.

Coronation necklace

Made for Queen Victoria in 1858 by Garrard & Co, the coronation necklace comprises 25 cushion diamonds with the 22.48-carat Lahore diamond as a pendant. Since 1902, it has been worn by every queen at their coronation and is one of the Queen's favourite pieces.

Queen Elizabeth II's armills

The Queen's solid gold ceremonial bracelets, known as armills, were a coronation gift from the Commonwealth and intended to replace the old pair, which had been in use since 1661. The bracelets represent sincerity and wisdom as well as being symbolic of the bond between the sovereign and their people.

The orb

The Sovereign's Orb was made for the coronation of Charles II in 1661 and represents the Christian world. Made from solid gold and weighing 2.6 pounds, it is decorated with 375 pearls, 365 diamonds, 18 rubies, nine emeralds, nine sapphires, one amethyst and one piece of glass.

The Robe of State

Elizabeth II's heavy purple velvet Robe of State was specially made for her coronation by the royal robe makers Ede & Ravenscroft and follows strict guidelines which stipulate that the train should be six yards long, trimmed with ermine and decorated with gold embroidery.

The gown

The Queen's white satin gown was designed by Norman Hartnell and took eight months to create, using British silk, which was painstakingly decorated with the embroidered floral emblems of Britain and the Commonwealth and then embellished with thousands of diamanté, crystals and seed pearls.

Coronation festivities

Almost a decade on since the end of World War II, Britain was still suffering from the after-effects of conflict, but the prospect of a royal coronation breathed new life into an exhausted nation; it symbolised a new start. Across the Commonwealth, festivals, street parties and celebrations were organised. Despite the fact that many food staples were still rationed, Churchill relaxed the regulations to enable caterers and revellers to celebrate.

— *2 June 1953* —

Winston Churchill and Queen
Elizabeth II had a close relationship
during his tenure as prime minister

WINSTON AND THE
WINDSORS

Forever remembered for his wartime leadership, Churchill's close ties with the royal family also helped to shape the future of a nation

Words by **Charles Ginger**

Brash. Bombastic. Brilliant. No summary of the character of Britain's greatest wartime leader would be accurate without these adjectives. Yet while the very mention of Winston Churchill is enough to conjure up a spirit of determination and images of a cigar-puffing old bulldog barking orders and giving everyone around him the two fingers (not always as a sign of his faith in victory), the charismatic son of Lord Randolph Churchill and Jennie Jerome also had a private, gentle, affectionate side that very few people were ever privileged enough to see. Some of those who did were the British royal family.

As a man who cherished until his dying breath both the sustenance of a monarchy and the 'golden' years of the British Empire, it may be no surprise that Churchill became very close to King George VI during WWII, a global struggle that threatened the continued existence of both ideas. Yet while the two eventually became firm friends, their bond was far from inevitable. In fact, in June 1939, just a few months prior to the start of WWII, King George confided in the Canadian prime minister at the time, William Mackenzie King, that he "would never wish to appoint Churchill to any offices unless it were absolutely necessary in time of war".

History tells us that King George was obliged to do just that in May 1940 as Britain looked set to

be invaded by the rampant forces of Nazi Germany. While his reservations about Churchill's suitably for the role have been well recorded - the calamity of the Gallipoli Campaign during WWI being one cause - his emerging respect for Churchill, which developed as the conflict progressed, is equally as well documented. It was a grudging admiration that would one day see both men regard the other with genuine affection.

After the triumphant conclusion of WWII, during which King George had met with Churchill every Tuesday afternoon for lunch and conversations of all kinds, Britain's reigning monarch and much-loved prime minister remained close during what was a turbulent time for the Tory leader.

By 1945 Britain had not held a general election for almost ten years, a hiatus caused by the war and the country's political parties agreeing to form a coalition for the duration of the conflict. Safe in the knowledge that Germany had by now been soundly defeated, the Labour Party no longer deemed it beneficial to uphold this temporary agreement, a move that encouraged Churchill to tender his resignation as prime minister on 23 May. However, Churchill's political relief would be short-lived, for on the very same day his king and long-time ally invited him to form what would become known as the Churchill Caretaker Ministry.

As the leader of this new government, Churchill continued to act as Britain's prime minister until the July election. To the amazement of his many supporters, Churchill lost the election, with Clement Atlee's Labour Party securing 47.7 per cent of the popular vote. Having been Britain's undisputed and hugely admired leader for five trying years, Churchill now confronted the prospect of being reduced to the leader of the Opposition, a position he would hold for six years. On 27 July he chaired his final cabinet meeting before stepping aside as prime minister. As the ministers made to leave the room at the conclusion of the meeting, Churchill turned to his understudy and a man who served him loyally throughout the war, Anthony Eden, and sighed, "Thirty years of my life have been passed in this room. I shall never sit in it again. You will, but I shall not."

Now in his 70s, Churchill had been on the nation's radar for approaching half a century, his political career enjoying many intoxicating highs and just as many crushing lows. Yet the political arena was not the only stage on which he conducted himself with aplomb. As adroit with royalty as he was with political rivals, Churchill had begun to establish a firm friendship with King George's eldest daughter, Elizabeth.

The man who would lead Britain through its darkest hours first encountered the child who

A thoughtful Churchill accompanies King George and his wife on a tour of Blitz wreckage in London

"BRITAIN'S FUTURE MONARCH CLEARLY MADE QUITE AN IMPRESSION ON CHURCHILL"

would become the longest-reigning living monarch in history while visiting the king and his queen consort, Elizabeth Bowes-Lyon, at their country estate of Balmoral in Scotland in September 1928. Churchill was immediately taken with two-year-old Elizabeth; in a letter he penned to his wife, Clementine, Churchill was effusive in his praise for the future queen: "She is a character. She has an air of authority and reflectiveness astonishing in an infant."

Britain's future monarch clearly made quite an impression on then-chancellor Churchill, and although she of course would have been too young to have ever recalled their first meeting, Elizabeth would have many more opportunities to impress Churchill as an adult. In fact, such was the devotion that she would come to inspire in Churchill, many members of staff and historians have commented on his love of the Queen.

Evidently keen to both help and protect Princess Elizabeth, in 1947, when Jock Colville, Churchill's private secretary during WWII, was approached about performing the same role for Elizabeth, Churchill was adamant that Colville simply had to accept the post. "It is your duty to accept," he informed the long-time aide.

On 9 July of the same year Elizabeth, now 21, announced her engagement to Philip Mountbatten. Delighted by the news of an impending royal wedding and eager to congratulate a young princess with whom he had become close, Churchill was one of the first well-wishers to write to the family. His glowing letter to King George so moved Elizabeth that she replied to it with a handwritten note to thank Churchill for a letter that had "touched me deeply".

Away from his regular encounters with the royals, Churchill had proven no less of a force on

the political circuit. Addressing the Primrose League (a branch of the Conservative Party) at a gathering in the Albert Hall shortly before the announcement of the royal engagement, Churchill had spoken once more of a 'united Europe', a pioneering concept that he had mentioned in a speech in Zurich, Switzerland, in 1946. On that occasion he had reiterated a long-held desire to see France and Germany establish a bond that would prevent them from once again waging war on each other. However, while he was a key supporter of what he described as a "kind of United States of Europe", Churchill was steadfast in his belief that Britain should remain outside of such a bloc.

"Great Britain, the British Commonwealth of Nations, mighty America, and I trust Soviet Russia, for then indeed all would be well, must be the friends and sponsors of the new Europe and must champion its right to live and shine."

Such was Churchill's influence on the European political scene, given his role in helping to defeat Nazi Germany, that his speeches on European unity helped to mobilise governments on the continent into forming the Council of Europe. This was despite the fact that he obstinately opposed any moves to link Britain to the emerging European ties.

Churchill in his element addressing a crowd, this time at a Women Conservatives meeting in 1954

Churchill enjoys some rare down time painting a scenic view in France while on holiday

As for the state of play in Britain as 1947 drew to a close, the mood was one of careful optimism, a reserved sense of life improving that was helped by a looming royal wedding. On 20 November Princess Elizabeth and Philip Mountbatten became husband and wife in a service at Westminster Abbey that was attended by a host of royals, nobles and political figures, among them Churchill and his wife. More happy news followed almost exactly a year later with the birth of the couple's first child, Charles, on 14 November 1948.

While attending regal events, meeting with prominent movers and shakers and continuing his work in opposition no doubt invigorated Churchill, they also began to take their toll on him. In 1949,

while on holiday in France with Clementine, Churchill suffered a minor stroke. Unsurprisingly considering his determined nature, he refused to let it prevent him from carrying out his duties or attending to other, more private necessities, such as acknowledging a key milestone in Princess Elizabeth's life. On the first anniversary of Prince Charles's birth Churchill sent his wishes once more to the royals. Elizabeth promptly responded with a telegram to thank him, further evidence of their strengthening relationship. It wouldn't be long before Elizabeth and Churchill were required to be in more regular official communication.

Despite resigning in 1945 in the wake of his election defeat, Churchill had not handed the

mantle of Tory leadership over to Anthony Eden, even though many had expected him to do so. As a result, he found himself well placed to contest the next general election, held in 1950. Although Labour won again, this time they did so by just six seats. With such a small majority, the party deemed it necessary to call a snap election just 20 months later. The decision backfired spectacularly as the Tory Party claimed 321 seats. Churchill was back in Number 10.

Seismic news of a very different nature was to follow in 1952, a development that was deeply upsetting not just for Churchill personally but also the royal family and the nation as a whole. It was well known within King George's private circles that Britain's monarch had not been well since the war, a conflict he was unexpectedly forced to guide the nation through in the wake of his brother Edward's abdication in 1936 - a decision, incidentally, that Churchill supported, in direct opposition to George.

Now in his early 50s, George's health was failing fast, little helped by his habit of smoking heavily, a routine that led to lung cancer and the subsequent partial removal of the affected organ. Other ailments, including a blockage in his right leg that

A VERY TROUBLING SUGGESTION

Concerned by the growth of the USSR, in 1946 Churchill encouraged President Truman to do the unthinkable

A key geopolitical subject that often occupied Churchill's mind during his spell in opposition was the growing threat of the Soviet Union. In a now famous speech made in 1946 while visiting the United States, Churchill lamented the expansion of the eastern powerhouse: "From Stettin in the Baltic to Trieste in the Adriatic, an Iron Curtain has descended across the continent. Behind that line lie all the capitals of the ancient states

of Central and Eastern Europe. Warsaw, Berlin, Prague, Vienna, Budapest, Belgrade, Bucharest and Sofia, all these famous cities and the populations around them lie in what I must call the Soviet sphere."

Astoundingly given his unique insight into the unimaginable horrors of war, such was Churchill's yearning to prevent Stalin from gaining any more influence on global affairs that he suggested to US President Truman

in a 1947 memo that America launch a nuclear attack on Moscow before it could acquire its own nuclear arsenal. Thankfully, Truman rejected the idea.

According to a member of the FBI, Churchill reiterated his apocalyptic idea in 1947, saying that "the only salvation for the civilisation of the world would be if the President of the United States would declare Russia to be imperilling world peace and attack Russia".

Churchill shakes hands with Truman and Stalin. He would later encourage the former to obliterate the latter

'KEEP ENGLAND WHITE'

With immigrants arriving in the UK to help rebuild a war-ravaged nation, Churchill sought to foment a racist backlash

It is beyond contention that throughout his political life Winston Churchill often courted controversy, and his policies on race in the 1950s are arguably one of the most outrageous chapters in his mixed legacy.

Concerned by the influx of immigrants in the 1950s, and with a General Election looming in 1955, Churchill (as has been revealed by recently unearthed cabinet papers) aired his apprehension in a cabinet meeting on 3 February 1954. According to the notes he warned his ministers that "problems will arise if many coloured people settle here. Are we to saddled ourselves with colour problems in the UK? [They are] attracted by [the] welfare state. Public opinion won't stand for it."

As the election approached, he went further by suggesting that the Conservative Party run on a ticket of 'Keep England White', a blatant bid to whip up public anxiety and thereby resentment towards the foreign workers who had been previously welcomed.

Believed by some historians to have been of the view that the white race stood above all others, Churchill was recorded on numerous occasions making other inflammatory racial remarks, such as when he lamented, "I hate Indians. They are a beastly people with a beastly religion."

While it is worth noting that Churchill was espousing opinions widely held at the time, such an acknowledgment does nothing to lessen the abhorrence of said beliefs. Britain's wartime saviour was truly a man of two sides.

Thousands of West Indian migrants were invited to the UK in a bid to replenish a depleted labour force

A visibly ailing Churchill is photographed in his usual attire during the final years of his life

"GEORGE DISMISSED THE OPINIONS OF HIS DOCTORS"

could have resulted in an amputation, meant that the king was no longer fit to journey around the Commonwealth as he had done. Dutiful as ever and deeply conscious of her role as the heir presumptive, Princess Elizabeth filled in for her father on numerous occasions. In a cruel twist of irony, it would be Elizabeth's performance of her royal duties that ultimately led to George's death, though through no fault of her own.

Adamant that he was going to bid his daughter and son-in-law farewell at London Airport on the morning of 31 January 1952 before they departed for Kenya, their first stop en route to a tour of Australia, George dismissed the opinions of his doctors and headed for the airport. The journey exerted an already exhausted king, and on 6 February he was found dead at Sandringham House having passed in his sleep. He was only 56.

While the news of King George's death did not come as a complete shock, it still devastated those close to him, none more so than Churchill. Upon

hearing of the king's passing Churchill burst into tears, and when Jock Colville went to visit him later on, he found Churchill in a cloud of despair: "When I went to the PM's bedroom, he was sitting alone with tears in his eyes looking straight ahead of him. I had not realised how much the king had meant to him."

This vulnerable episode in Churchill's private life also gave rise to a rather strange comment when Colville attempted to console his friend. "I tried to cheer him up by saying how well he would get on with the new queen," recalled Colville, "but all he could say was that he did not know her, and that she was only a child."

Whether Churchill simply said this in a moment of total grief or he actually did genuinely feel as though he barely knew the brand-new monarch, what is beyond doubt is that they would come to know each other very well. Furthermore, he must have felt he knew Elizabeth fairly well given what he did next.

Churchill welcomes Queen Elizabeth to a
retirement dinner held the night before he
stepped down as prime minister in April 1955

Intervening in the affairs of others had never been something that Churchill baulked at, and with Elizabeth's coronation approaching he readied to do so once more. As had been the long-standing tradition in royal families, it was widely anticipated that the new royal couple would adopt Philip's family name, Mountbatten, upon Elizabeth's accession to the throne. Unfortunately for Philip, an influential figure favoured the retention of the title Windsor, and Churchill was supported in this notion by none other than Elizabeth's own mother. On 9 April 1952 Elizabeth made it known publicly that she would remain a Windsor.

It is clear from Elizabeth's adherence to Churchill's advice that the young ruler regarded her prime minister with the utmost respect, but the two were also bound in less austere ways, chief among them a mutual love of horses and racing. A lunch at Hurst Park Racecourse in May 1951 highlighted just how much Elizabeth and Churchill had in common. At the racecourse to watch the Winston Churchill Stakes, Elizabeth invited the race's namesake for lunch before the

event got underway. Both parties had a vested interest in the outcome - Elizabeth's horse, Above Board, would be competing against Churchill's, Colonist II. It would be the latter horse who eventually triumphed, pushing Elizabeth's into second place.

Official meetings between the pair were also often enjoyable occasions, and by necessity following Elizabeth's ascension in 1952, became more frequent as the new queen - still only in her mid-20s - sought her prime minister's counsel on domestic and global affairs. Members of the Queen's staff would later recall hearing "peals of laughter" from inside their meeting rooms and seeing Churchill departing with tears in his eyes. Even so, not all of their discussions were of a cheerful nature, especially during the winter of 1952 when London found itself suffocated in a cloud of pollution that became known as the Great Smog for five choking days.

Precipitated by a period of unusually cold weather and the inevitable rush to light fires in order to keep homes warm and factories producing goods as normal throughout England's

capital, the blanket of fog that descended on 5 December at first seemed unremarkable. But as the day wore on and the clouds adopted a sickly yellow hue it became apparent that something serious was unfolding. Toxins from factory furnaces and domestic chimneys were mixing with the mist and thereby dispersing a poisonous fog throughout the city. By the time it eventually lifted on 10 December, hundreds of people - most of them young, elderly or suffering from pre-existing respiratory problems - lay dead, a figure that eventually rose to 4,000 in the weeks and months after. Some studies have since suggested that as many as 12,000 lives were prematurely ended by the smog.

Churchill has been accused in recent times of showing little interest in the event or concern for its many victims, but there is thought to be little evidence to support this claim. After all, it seems highly unlikely that a weather event that claimed so many lives and caused travel chaos throughout London (boats on the Thames could not sail, flights were grounded due to poor visibility and trains stopped running for the same reason)

The former prime minister enjoys tea with his wife and a canine companion at Chartwell House

would have provoked anything but concern for Churchill, or for the ministers in his government, especially so soon after the war.

An event that certainly invoked a great deal of worry for Churchill personally and his friends and family was his second stroke, suffered on 23 June 1953, just three weeks after Elizabeth's coronation. As guests were filing out of a dinner held at Number 10 for the Italian prime minister, Churchill was seen - fortunately only by his closest aides - to slump forwards in his chair. Remarkably they managed to usher him safely out of the room without anyone else realising that something was seriously wrong with him.

Mounting a characteristic counter-attack against such problems, Churchill insisted on leading the following morning's Cabinet meeting, and his determination to avoid the news of his ill health leaking to the public was understandable. A publicly weakened Winston Churchill would have represented an easy target for political adversaries wishing to oust him once and for all. Yet, while Fleet Street agreed to keep quiet out of a sense of deep loyalty to Churchill, those around the ailing prime minister could see the impact his latest stroke had made, including the Queen.

Aware that his health was slowly fading, Churchill did his best to put off retirement for as long as he could, but by 1955 it was evident he would need to step down. This he finally did on 5 April, standing aside one last time to make room for Eden at the age of 80.

Although he had been forced from Number 10 much sooner than he would have liked, by the following year he admitted to his personal physician, Charles Wilson, "I am not the man I was. I could not be prime minister now."

It appears that Queen Elizabeth was also becoming increasingly aware of Churchill's

The content of Churchill and the Queen's conversation fails to engage a young Prince Charles, 1953

"FEW WERE AS MOVED BY HIS LOSS AS QUEEN ELIZABETH"

decline, going so far in 1957 as to discuss with the newly elected prime minister Harold MacMillan that when the time came, Churchill was to be afforded a state funeral. This was to be in recognition of his wartime services.

The day in question came on 24 January 1965, when Churchill, having suffered another stroke just nine days before, passed away at his home in London at the age of 90. The man who had led the nation with grit and wit was duly afforded the state funeral that the Queen had promised. In recognition of her affection for him, she even broke royal protocol by arriving at the ceremony at St Paul's Cathedral before both the coffin and the Churchill family and then leaving long after them, a reversal of the usual process that deeply touched Churchill's relatives. The level of gratitude and genuine love for Churchill was there for all to see in a ceremony that was as awe-inspiring as the man himself. His widow Clementine beautifully summed up the funeral when she beamed, "This wasn't a funeral, it was a triumph."

Few were as moved by the loss of Churchill as Queen Elizabeth, for he had been a guiding light and cheering friend throughout her formative years. He in turn had served her with nothing short of absolute devotion. Some have suggested that she was not as fond of him as he was of her, but when asked years later who her favourite prime minister had been, the Queen's answer provided a rebuttal to this claim that Churchill would surely have grinned at: "Winston, of course, because it was always such fun."

A seemingly endless line of mourners pass the coffin of Churchill as he lies in state in St Paul's Cathedral, January 1965

Images © Getty

Churchill's birthday portrait

To commemorate the 80th birthday of the celebrated war-time leader Winston Churchill, members of the Houses of Parliament commissioned artist Graham Sutherland to paint a portrait, which was officially presented to him at Westminster Hall. Churchill cooly remarked that it was a "remarkable example of modern art", to the titters of MPs. Both Churchill and his wife, Clementine, famously despised the portrait, and it was hidden away at Churchill's country home of Chartwell. After the death of Clementine in 1978, it became abundantly clear that she had arranged for the portrait to be destroyed almost immediately by her public secretary, Grace Hamblin.

—— *30 November 1954* ——

In public the couple beamed for the cameras, but candid photographs reveal how exhausting their cheery facade was

TROUBLE AND
STRIFE

While the marriage of the handsome naval officer Philip Mountbatten to Princess Elizabeth seemed to be a perfect royal romance, tensions simmered beneath the surface

Words by **Melanie Clegg**

"I'm either being very brave or very stupid," the young naval officer Philip of Greece told his cousin Patricia Mountbatten over breakfast on the morning of his wedding, prompting her to consider later that "everything was going to change for him, he was giving up his freedom. He is quite intelligent enough to have foreseen a lot of the problems from his point of view, but thank God he did marry her."

To outsiders, dazzled by this most charming royal romance between a handsome and brave young prince and a pretty and dutiful princess, who was very much considered to be the sweetheart of the nation, Philip was nothing less than the luckiest man on Earth to have captured such a precious and rare prize as the heir to the British throne. The attempts by certain newspapers to whip up ill feeling against the prince by reminding readers of his unfortunate close family connections to members of the Nazi Party, his relative impoverishment and the fact that his family's chequered history over recent years had left him curiously lacking in both official country and surname until he adopted that of his uncle and mentor Lord Mountbatten, only served to reinforce the fairytale nature of the romance and increase sympathy for the young prince, left dispossessed and rootless like so many others had been after the recent end of the Second World War. Despite strong links to Germany thanks to the fact that all four of his sisters had married into the German aristocracy, the fact that Philip courageously served with the Royal Navy during the Second World War only served to increase public sympathy for the match - even if his three surviving sisters were not invited to the wedding in case their presence there caused an unpleasant furore.

Unfortunately for Philip, the lukewarm press coverage of the royal engagement echoed the serious misgivings of the close knit circle of officials, dubbed 'the moustaches' by Philip's sister-in-law Princess Margaret and headed by the intimidating private secretary Tommy Lascelles, that surrounded the royal family, who believed that Philip - with his links to the Nazis, unstable family history and lack of money or assets - was not a suitably impressive partner for a future queen. Philip's blunt and occasionally insensitive manner, tactlessness and rough sense of humour were also considered problematic by courtiers, who were often scandalised by the brusquely forthright way that he spoke to his fiancée. Her parents were more willing to take all of this in their stride, not least because Princess Elizabeth's father had once been a naval officer himself and shared his prospective son-in-law's sense of humour and boisterous love of practical jokes, but nonetheless felt that they wanted someone quite different for their precious eldest daughter.

The royal couple were very much in favour of Princess Elizabeth marrying one of the titled, wealthy young men that she had known all of her

The couple's 1953 Commonwealth tour was a great success, but it put a huge strain on their marriage

"THE FACT THAT PHILIP SERVED WITH THE ROYAL NAVY INCREASED SYMPATHY"

life, such as Lord Porchester, heir to Earl Caernarvon, who shared her passion for horses and racing and would one day inherit Highclere Castle and thousands of acres of land. Compared to Porchester and the other aristocratic prospective candidates for Princess Elizabeth's hand, Philip - despite his royal bloodline, education at a British boarding school, descent from Queen Victoria and stellar military service - was considered to be an outsider and as such he was treated with suspicion.

The reservations of her family and their circle did nothing to deter Princess Elizabeth, however, who had set her heart on Philip and was

determined to marry him no matter what. Although his fiancée's faith in him naturally did much to boost Philip's confidence, he could not help but be aware that his presence in the royal family was not exactly welcomed with open arms by their circle, and this resentment on both sides, set the tone not just for his dealings with the palace administration but also, on occasion, Princess Elizabeth too, whose deep-seated desire to please everyone and do her duty often put her at odds with her husband.

When Philip and Elizabeth married in November 1947, George VI was only in his early 50s and they naturally expected him to live for

Prince Philip often felt overshadowed and sidelined, but the excited reception by this crowd of children shows that he was nonetheless popular in his own right

several more decades, enabling them to enjoy a relatively normal existence until the time came for Elizabeth to ascend the throne, which might not happen until she and Philip were in their fifties themselves. Philip was deeply committed to his naval career, which had given him a purpose and direction entirely unrelated to his marriage and association with the royal family, and hoped to remain in the Royal Navy for as long as possible before the king's death and the succession of his wife to the throne would force him to give it up.

Sadly his hopes were doomed to disappointment when his father-in-law died in February 1952 while Philip and Princess Elizabeth were on tour in Africa. When his friend Mike Parker informed him of the king's death, Philip looked, so Parker later recalled, "as if you'd dropped half the world on him". For Philip, his wife's succession to the throne marked the end of his naval career and the beginning of a long period during which he struggled to find his place in the royal hierarchy, which was made especially difficult by the fact that he felt like he had already given up everything in order to accommodate the exacting and sometimes contradictory requirements of both his wife and the establishment that she headed.

"HE FELT USURPED FROM HIS POSITION AS EVERYONE DEFERRED TO THE QUEEN"

Until Elizabeth's accession, Philip had been able to feel as though he was head of his own household and had very much enjoyed refurbishing Clarence House to transform it into their first family home - now, they were being forced to move to Buckingham Palace and he felt usurped from his position as everyone in the household deferred to the new monarch while he was made to feel like something of an inconvenience. "There were plenty of people telling me what not to do," Philip recalled later. "I had to try to support the Queen as best I could without getting in the way. The difficulty was to find things that might be useful."

Controversy about what the new royal family would call itself only served to add to Philip's unhappiness. When news broke that his uncle Lord Mountbatten had toasted the "royal house of Mountbatten" at a private dinner party just two

days after George VI's death, the royal family, headed by the Queen's formidable grandmother Queen Mary, were scandalised, while the prime minister Winston Churchill was furious and immediately sought the support of his Cabinet, who backed him up with an agreement that the royal family's name should remain Windsor. Philip wasn't entirely keen on changing the royal house's name to Mountbatten either and suggested 'Edinburgh and Windsor' as a compromise, only for this to also be dismissed by Churchill and the old guard, much to his annoyance.

The Queen found herself in a difficult position as she wanted to please her husband, especially as she was well aware of how much he had given up for her sake, including his beloved career in the Navy, but at the same time, she wished to do what was right and was forced to agree that retaining the Windsor name was for the best. When she

While Prince Philip loved and supported his wife, for the first years of their marriage he found it difficult to find his feet and often felt undermined and ignored

THE THURSDAY CLUB

As Prince Philip began to feel increasingly stifled and frustrated by his royal duties, he found much-needed breathing space at the weekly meetings of a rather rakish men's club in Soho

In 1947, shortly before his wedding to Princess Elizabeth, Prince Philip met the sophisticated society photographer Stirling Henry Nahum, who was known simply as 'Baron', at one of his uncle Lord Mountbatten's house parties at Broadlands and had liked him so much that he asked him to take the official photographs for his wedding later that year. In return, Baron invited the young prince to join his new private men's luncheon club, which met every Thursday afternoon in the second-floor dining room of Wheeler's fish restaurant on Old Compton Road in Soho. There, Philip, always attended by his close friend and private secretary Michael Parker, hobnobbed with a wide variety of aristocrats, writers, actors, artists and politicians, including celebrities like Peter Ustinov and David Niven, who were waited on by a gaggle of attractive young waitresses. Although meetings were veiled with secrecy, it was rumoured in the press that the meetings were no better than 'rip roaring stag parties', although members would later strenuously deny that anything improper ever took place and it was more about men larking about and playing silly pranks than anything more nefarious. Whatever the truth, it's certain that the club and its members offered Philip a valuable respite from his stressful royal duties.

The society photographer Baron was the founder of the famously secretive Thursday Club

announced in April that her family - in particular, the couple's offspring - would continue to bear the name of Windsor, Philip was crushed and felt deeply wounded by the snub. "I am the only man in the country not allowed to give his name to his children," he protested. "I'm nothing but a bloody amoeba". His aunt, Lady Mountbatten, later recalled that "it hurt him, it really hurt him. He had given up everything - and now came this, the final insult. It was a terrible blow. It upset him very deeply and left him feeling unsettled and unhappy for a long while".

The incident set the tone for their relationship for quite some time to come - although on the surface Philip offered his wholehearted support to his wife as she came to grips with her new position, behind the scenes he was feeling ignored, humiliated and insecure, and it's therefore no surprise that tensions often arose between the pair, usually in situations where Philip felt like his authority as head of the family was being challenged, such as in the question of where their children were to be educated.

Although most of the conflict played out in the privacy of the couple's apartments in the royal residences, still tensions were obvious to those who knew the couple well, such as Philip's close friend and private secretary Michael Parker, who was privy to what went on behind the palace's closed doors and knew how unhappy his friend was. Nonetheless, on at least one occasion, there were other witnesses to the crisis, such as when an Australian camera crew waiting to film the couple during their Commonwealth tour in early 1954 were shocked to see Philip run out of the house that they were staying in, closely followed by a hurled tennis racquet, his shoes and then his wife, who was loudly demanding that he come back indoors. One of the crew filmed the incident but then exposed the film and handed the tape over, much to the Queen's relief. The couple spent two months in Australia, covering thousands of miles in the process and having barely any time to themselves in between long days filled with

This photograph of Prince Philip and his close friend and private secretary Michael Parker was taken in Gibraltar on the day that they parted company as a result of the scandal surrounding Parker's divorce

"TENSIONS WERE OBVIOUS TO THOSE WHO KNEW THEM"

THE MOUNTBATTENS

One of the first disputes involved the naming of the royal house

The Battenberg family's close association with the British royal family began in 1851 when Queen Victoria's son-in-law, the Grand Duke of Hesse-Darmstadt, bestowed the title of Countess of Battenberg on his younger brother's morganatic wife, Julia Hauke. This connection would become cemented when Julia's son Henry married Victoria's youngest daughter Princess Beatrice and another son, Louis, married his cousin Princess Victoria of Hesse-Darmstadt, the eldest sister of Empress Alexandra Feodorovna of

Russia. Victoria and Louis' daughter Alice was mother to Prince Philip, while their son Louis would later become Earl Mountbatten. The family changed their name to the more Anglican sounding Mountbatten during WWI at the same time as George V decreed that the royal house should become Windsor. Much later, Lord Mountbatten's nephew Philip adopted the surname when he became a naturalised British subject and it was as Philip Mountbatten that he married Princess Elizabeth in 1947. However, when Elizabeth

succeeded to the throne, he and his family were disappointed when she gave in to pressure to retain Windsor as the royal house's name rather than change it to that of her husband. Nonetheless, shortly before the birth of Prince Andrew in 1960, the Queen decreed that the name Mountbatten-Windsor should be used by male line descendants of the couple who hold no other royal titles and styles. The first royal child to officially use the name was Princess Louise, daughter of Prince Edward and Sophie Rhys-Jones, who was born in 2003.

Prince Philip's uncle Lord Mountbatten was disappointed when the Queen refused to change the royal house's name

Rumours that Prince Philip was having an affair with the actress Pat Kirkwood lingered for several years, even though the pair were almost certainly just friends

official functions, speeches and parades so it's not surprising that they were feeling stressed out and that all the underlying tensions about Philip's role simmered to the surface.

Two years later, Philip returned to Australia in order to open the 1956 Olympic Games in Melbourne and this time he came alone, leaving Elizabeth and their two children behind in Britain. Philip's Commonwealth tour, which covered nearly 40,000 miles and took him to such distant outposts as Antarctica, New Guinea and Sri Lanka (then known as Ceylon), lasted for over four months and was described by the press back home as a 'stag do' and 'Philip's Folly', with rumours that Philip and his all-male entourage, which included the ubiquitous Michael Parker, and crew of sailors on the Royal Yacht Britannia were indulging in non-stop partying during the trip. The fact that Philip and Elizabeth could only communicate in the most rudimentary way via occasional telephone calls, telegrams and letters only served to make matters worse as the pair felt increasingly cut off from each other, not just by the physical distance between them.

Matters reached a head when Parker's wife, Eileen, filed for divorce while they were away, citing his adultery, which naturally led to much scurrilous speculation about Philip's private life and a revival of old gossip about the exclusive gentlemen's luncheon club, The Thursday Club, that both men were members of and which was suspected by some to be a den of orgiastic, drunken iniquity.

There is a tendency for rumours to start flying when a couple spend a lot of time apart, and when that couple is royal and already subject to intense scrutiny, people are especially keen to find evidence of adultery. It was well known that Philip had had a number of girlfriends before his marriage, including the glamorous American starlet Cobina Wright and Canadian socialite Osla Benning, and when news of the Parkers' divorce broke, it didn't take long before stories that he was still romantically dallying with a variety of society beauties, such as actresses Hélène Cordet and Pat Kirkwood, both of whom were known to be his friends, began to do the rounds, even though there was absolutely no proof that he had done

any such thing and indeed was reportedly very hurt and angry about the allegations.

In the end, the Queen was forced to take the unprecedented measure of issuing an official rebuttal, insisting that "it is quite untrue that there is any rift between the Queen and the Duke." Nonetheless, rumours about Philip's alleged infidelity would continue to resurface but never again would they be quite so virulent. For Philip, his epic voyage across the world had been a sobering experience that reminded him that he was no longer a carefree naval officer, used to spending several months at a time at sea, but instead a husband and father with duties and responsibilities at home. For the Queen too, it marked a definite change in their relationship. Within weeks of their reunion in Portugal, she had rewarded Philip by officially investing him with the title of Prince of the United Kingdom, which greatly increased his standing both at home and overseas as well as making him rather more of an equal than he had previously been in their marriage, and in the process healing many of the old hurts and rifts.

Philip with penguins

On his world tour of 1956-97, the Duke of Edinburgh became the first member of the royal family to travel into the Antarctic Circle. Returning from Australia, the Duke had travelled to the Falkland Islands to spend several days visiting the British stations, and during this trip he visited several Antarctic islands, including Deception Island and Adelaide Island. During one of his visits, he came upon a colony of emperor penguins. By the end of February, the Duke's tour was over.

— January 1957 —

Prince Charles was the first royal in British history to attend university, where he studied anthropology, archaeology and history at Cambridge

A PRINCE IN
TURMOIL

For young Prince Charles, school offered little emotional relief from his oppressed and lonely childhood

Words by **Philippa Grafton**

In Gordonstoun, a young, troubled Prince Philip found the closest thing to home he had ever known. During a period defined by war, anguish and a divided family, Philip sought refuge at the strict, disciplinarian boarding school, which provided him with stability, structure and unity. It's little wonder, then, that when it came to his own children's education mere decades later, Philip turned back to the school that had saved him from the tragic reality of his own childhood. But where Philip thrived under the strict regime, Prince Charles cracked and crumbled under the pressure.

The firstborn son of Princess Elizabeth and her husband, Prince Charles was born on 14 November 1948, just six days shy of his parents' first wedding anniversary. While the pregnancy had passed without serious incident, Charles's birth was not an easy one. Princess Elizabeth was in labour for 30 hours before she was sedated and doctors opted to deliver the baby via caesarean section. Agitated by the long labour, Philip had been restlessly pacing around Buckingham Palace waiting impatiently for news until his private secretary, Michael Parker, insisted on playing a game of squash to take their minds off the birth. When the word reached Philip that the baby had

finally been delivered, he sprinted to Elizabeth's bedside, bundled the newborn into his arms and declared that he looked like a "plum pudding". For the first few weeks of his life, Prince Charles was never far from his mother; the baby slept in the dressing room that joined the princess's bedroom, and she happily breast-fed her newborn, until she suffered a bout of measles in January 1949 and she was separated from her baby, handing him into the care of nannies and nurses.

This premature separation marked the first of many partings and disappointments for the young Prince Charles. With his father a celebrated naval officer and his mother the heir to the British throne, Charles's parents struggled to give their new child the attention that he so craved. Princess Elizabeth was determined to see her son daily; at 9am, the young boy would be brought to see his mother, and in the evenings - assuming her busy schedule allowed it - she would head to the nursery to spend time with her son before bedtime. Despite this, motherhood had put additional strain on an already stretched princess - not only was she expected to perform royal duties befitting a future queen, but she was a devoted daughter to her increasingly frail father, and a loving wife to her husband, whose career

was on the cusp of greatness. An undisputed war hero, Philip had shown great promise in his naval career, and it was expected that one day he would secure the coveted role of First Sea Lord. He was devoted to his job and was hellbent on achieving as much as possible before he would eventually be forced to give it all up upon the ascension of his wife.

The young couple were doggedly determined to live as normal a life as possible before the inevitable happened, and Philip's career called him out to Malta, where the pair resided for several months out of the year from 1949. In this peaceful Mediterranean haven, Philip and Elizabeth managed to live a remarkably normal life, with the princess taking up a position with the Soldiers, Sailors, Airmen and Families Association charity. For the young, in-love couple, these carefree days were bliss; for their young son, who remained in the care of nannies, nurses and his grandmother back in the UK, these were the foundation blocks for a relationship defined by difference and distance.

What the young prince lacked in parental affection from Princess Elizabeth and Philip, he made up for in his close bond with his grandmother. A sensitive child who craved

The Queen came to watch Prince Charles's first ever sports day at Hill House in July 1957

attention, Charles found the love he desired from the queen, who proved to be the young boy's closest companion throughout his childhood years. Although the queen had had a similarly distant relationship with her own children, usually only seeing them for mealtimes and before bed, Queen Elizabeth embraced her role as doting grandmother, indulging her grandson to the point of spoiling him. She cultivated the young boy's passion for the arts, showing him the Royal Collection's finest paintings and allowing him to explore Windsor Castle. But in her lavish affection, Queen Elizabeth pandered to the young prince, which in turn encouraged Charles's bad habits, such as whingeing and self-pity. When he saw these traits in his son, Philip was so appalled that he sought to discipline them out of him.

Princess Anne, who had been born in the summer of 1950, was the polar opposite of her

brother - in many ways, Anne was the son that Philip had hoped Charles could be. Anne was independent and wilful, humorous and sporty. This rough-and-tumble tomboy quickly won her father's praise, something that Charles had craved.

In February 1952, the inevitable finally happened. King George VI passed away, leaving the throne to his eldest daughter. It was a moment that the whole family dreaded - Elizabeth and Philip were forced to sacrifice the happy lives they had built for themselves in Malta. From their English residence of Clarence House they moved into Buckingham Palace, and Philip, the former head of the family, way usurped by his wife, the newly named Queen Elizabeth II.

With this change came additional responsibilities for the couple. Only a matter of months after Elizabeth's coronation in June 1953, the pair set off on a six-month Commonwealth

tour. When they returned in the spring of 1954, they found their two children welcoming but aloof. According to the Queen years later, they "were terribly polite. I don't think they really knew who we were." In the months since their parents had gone away, the two children had continued to be brought up by nannies, the only difference to their daily lives the missing bedtime visits from their parents.

For the two young royals, their nannies had all but replaced their parents. Helen Lightbody loomed large in Prince Charles's childhood, running the nursery and taking care of the prince. It's rumoured that a young, inexperienced Elizabeth was fearful of the domineering older woman, who was as strict with Charles's mother as she was with the young boy. However, after allegedly incurring the wrath of the Queen in 1956, Lightbody was forced to resign. She was

Prince Charles was flown to Gordonstoun by his father

"THE ROYALS QUESTIONED THE YOUNG PRINCE'S FUTURE"

swiftly replaced by the younger Mabel Anderson, who eventually took care of all of the Queen and Philip's children. In 1953 the family hired Catherine Peebles as Charles's governess, tasked with taking charge of the future king's early education. Catherine wasn't new to tutoring royalty; her previous job had been with the Duke of Kent's children. The governess's approach to teaching her young charge was soft but encouraging - she understood the young child's disposition and offered him praise and encouragement for doing well rather than reprimanding him for mistakes.

Sadly, Charles's happy days with Catherine were limited. It was soon decided that what Prince Charles really needed was the company of other children, something he could only truly benefit from by attending school. With that in mind, the prince became a pupil at Hill House in Kensington

at the end of 1956. He became the first heir apparent to be sent to public school.

At Hill House, Prince Charles found himself treated like any of the school's other students. He was noted for enjoying drawing and painting, and he proved himself more than capable at reading and writing. He particularly excelled at music. What he struggled with, however, was maths. Although the young boy was only at the school for a few months, he attended the school's sports day at the end of the academic year in 1957, captured on film introducing his mother to his fellow pupils, who duly shook hands and bowed.

From Hill House, Prince Charles began to take his tentative first steps in the same direction as his father. In September 1957, Charles took up a place at Cheam School, a strict boarding school in Hampshire that Philip had attended. He struggled to make friends, instead finding himself a target to

the school's bullies, and was stricken by homesickness. His troubles at the school continued when, the following year, he was summoned to the headmaster's office with several other students. Here, the boys were allowed to watch the Commonwealth Games in Cardiff on the TV. In a speech made at the Games, the Queen revealed that she had decided to bequeath her son the title of Prince of Wales - a revelation that took the prince by surprise and embarrassment, especially when the boys in the room turned to him to congratulate him on his new status.

Life at Cheam continued much the same - with the very occasional caning for bad behaviour - but behind the scenes, the royal family were questioning Charles's future. With his time at Cheam drawing to a close, a decision needed to be made on where to send him next. Two schools caught the attention of the royals: Eton College in Windsor, or Gordonstoun in the north of Scotland. Both schools had vocal supporters, with Prince Philip backing his own alma mater, while the Queen Mother voiced her support for Eton, but the final decision lay with Queen Elizabeth. Ever her grandson's most supportive companion, the Queen Mother insisted that Charles should attend Eton, writing to the Queen in May 1961, "I have been thinking such a lot about Charles. I suppose that he will be taking his entrance exam for Eton soon. I do hope he passes because it might be the ideal school for one of his character and temperament. However good Gordonstoun is, it is miles and miles away and he might as well be at school abroad." Assured that her opinion could sway her daughter, she continued, "All of your friends' sons are at Eton and it is so important to be able to grow up with people you will be with later in life. And so nice and so important when boys are growing up that you and Philip can see him during school holidays and keep in touch with what is happening. He would be terribly cut off and lonely in the far north."

What the Queen Mother hadn't bargained for, however, was her son-in-law's determined grit and insistence on having some semblance of authority within his own family. Philip rebutted the Queen Mother's argument by claiming that Charles would be harassed by the media were he to go to Eton. What the boy needed was solitude and

With his parents often away, the young prince grew close to his grandmother, the Queen Mother

Images © Getty

Photographed here in 1958 while he attended Cheam School, Charles was mocked mercilessly for his protruding ears

Like Gordonstoun, Timbertop challenged the prince, but he felt more accepted there than at his previous schools

While studying at Gordonstoun, Charles indulged in his passion for drama, here playing Macbeth in the a 1965 rendition of the Shakespeare play

independence - at Gordonstoun, Charles would find himself and thrive, just as Philip had done three decades before. In the end, Elizabeth sided with her husband and Prince Charles's fate was sealed.

In May 1962, Prince Philip piloted a plane and flew his son to an RAF base near the school, then drove him to the gates of Gordonstoun. With the knowledge that the heir to the throne was about to attend this remote school, two or three boys who knew Charles had been enrolled at the school in an attempt to make the transition easier, but several rule changes at the school in the lead-up to the prince's arrival thwarted any chance Charles had of settling in comfortably. Misdemeanours that previously went unpunished or slipped under the radar, such as drinking and smoking, suddenly carried heavy penalties - being

caught smoking could result in a caning, while being caught drinking could lead to expulsion. Another rule that was forced upon students was that any antagonistic behaviour towards Prince Charles may result in expulsion.

Resentment mounted against the new pupil, and by the time he moved into his new accommodation in Windmill Lodge, he was the most despised student on campus. Any student seen being friendly towards the prince was mercilessly mocked, accused of sucking up to him. Despite the rule against mistreating him, Charles found himself once again a target for bullies, who allegedly attacked him in his sleep and verbally abused him. In February 1963, Charles wrote to his grandmother to exclaim, "I hate coming back here and leaving home; I hardly get any sleep at

the House because I snore and get hit on the head the whole time. It is absolute hell." Letter after letter followed, complaining of the cruelty the young prince suffered at the hands of his schoolmates. "He was crushingly lonely for most of his time there," recalled a fellow student years later. "The wonder is that he survived with his sanity intact."

For several years, Charles endured the trials and tribulations of Gordonstoun, finding occasional joy in the performing arts. In 1965, Prince Charles was elated to play the lead in *Macbeth*, which his parents came to see. To his bitter disappointment, Charles could hear his father's guffaws during one particularly emotive scene. Allegedly when the prince asked what his father was laughing at, Philip cuttingly replied, "It sounds like The Goons."

During his time at university, Charles indulged his passion for music by playing the cello for Trinity College's orchestra

THE 'CHERRY BRANDY' INCIDENT

How one wrong foot sent Charles spiralling back to square one

In his second year at Gordonstoun at the age of 14, Charles had the pleasure of joining the school's sailing team, where he experienced some semblance of freedom. However, the luxury was to be short-lived when one minor misdeed on an excursion catapulted to nationwide infamy.

Having sailed to Stornoway Harbour, the young crew were given permission to explore the shore. However, the sight of Britain's next king in town set tongues wagging, and a crowd quickly began to gather around Charles. While his protection officer, Donald Green, had gone to buy the boys cinema tickets, Charles sought refuge in a hotel, descending deeper into the building to hide away from the attention. The room he found himself in, however, proved to be a pub. When the bartender asked what he wanted to drink, Charles blurted out "Cherry brandy" – the "first drink that came into my head... because I'd drunk it before when it was cold out shooting," he later lamented. Unknown to the prince, however, a journalist happened to be seated nearby. This typical teenage rebellion made headline news the next day.

As punishment, Charles was stripped of his sailing privileges, and his protection officer who had supported the young prince throughout his terrible ordeal at Gordonstoun was fired. "I have never been able to forgive them for doing that because he defended me in the most marvellous way and he was the most wonderful, loyal, splendid man," Prince Charles retorted many decades later.

Prince Charles was stripped of his sailing privileges, but also his closest companion after underage drinking in Stornoway

"IN AUSTRALIA, CHARLES WAS JUST AN ORDINARY STUDENT"

In February 1966, Philip made the decision to send Charles to study in Australia for a few months. Charles was flown out to Geelong Grammar's Timbertop campus, a remote school which challenged him in new and more exciting ways than Gordonstoun. The school prided itself on challenging its students physically, encouraging them to take part in outdoor activities like chopping trees, camping and going on cross-country treks. With the teenager Philip had sent his equerry, David Checketts. Remarkably,

considering how badly Charles had settled in at his previous schools, he found life more than bearable in Australia. Here, fellow students and teachers cared little for Charles's title; he was just another ordinary student, and was treated as such. During the week he worked hard at school and made friends, while his weekends were spent with his father's equerry and family, enjoying some semblance of a normal life.

"I went out with a boy and came back with a man," David famously stated of the prince's

Australian sojourn. As well as finding himself, Charles's trip to Australia provided him with his first real taste of what it meant to be a royal. He performed his royal duties admirably, attending dozens of events and perfecting the art of talking to the crowds, as well as officials and politicians. When the time came to leave Timbertop, students gave a rousing cheer for the "real Pommy bastard" in typical friendly humour.

Despite his traumatic experiences at Gordonstoun, when Charles returned for his final

Stuart McGregor, a pupil at Timbertop, was assigned to welcome Prince Charles to the school. The pair became friends and kept in touch, reconnecting face to face at the old school in 2005

The Free Wales Army was a nationalist group determined to secure Welsh independence

"CHARLES WAS PRAISED FOR HIS DILIGENCE AND TALENTS"

year he found himself elected head boy, a surprise honour that nobody had really expected. With just months until his graduation from the school he'd so despised, the question once again arose about Charles's future. After some debate, it was decided that Charles would attend university – specifically Trinity College at Cambridge, where he chose to study anthropology, archaeology and history. In October 1967, Charles arrived at his new residence, a second-floor flat on campus. Next door stayed David Checketts, who had since been assigned as Charles's own equerry.

Charles might not have been as academically gifted as his fellow students, but he was praised for his diligence and talents by his tutors, and after his first year he was on track for a 2:1. What Charles truly loved, however, was acting, and he delved into the university's creative side with gusto. As well as joining the famous Footlights Dramatic Society, he took part in college theatrics

and joined Trinity College's orchestra where he played the cello. Despite embracing university life, Charles still longed to be outdoors. "Any excuse to escape Cambridge and plod across ploughed fields instead of stagnating in lecture rooms is enormously welcome," he wrote to a friend after attending a shoot in January 1969.

In anticipation of his investiture as Prince of Wales in 1969, Prince Charles was to be pulled out of Cambridge and sent to the University College of Wales in Aberystwyth to become acquainted with Welsh language and culture. However, unrest had spread throughout Wales in the run-up to the event, with a nationalist group called the Free Wales Army – modelled on the IRA – planting bombs across the country in the previous years. Succumbing to the threats of a terrorist organisation was not an option, however, and Prince Charles was duly sent to live at Pantycelyn Hall. Despite the chaos, Prince Charles threw

himself into understanding his new principality. He empathised with the Welsh, writing to a friend that "they are depressed by what might happen to [Wales] if they don't try and preserve the language and the culture, which is unique and special to Wales, and if something is unique and special, I see it as worth preserving." On 1 July 1969, Prince Charles's investiture was televised across the country. With the threat of a terrorist attack still very much a possibility, the ceremony went ahead, but with Prince Charles in bulletproof gear beneath his regalia.

In June 1970, Charles became the first British royal to earn a university degree when he graduated from Cambridge with a 2:2 Bachelor of Arts degree. With his formal education at an end, the prince was free to pursue a more traditional royal education: military service. In an interview with *The Observer* in the 70s, Prince Charles reflected on his years of school turmoil: "I didn't enjoy school as much as I might have, but that was only because I'm happier at home than anywhere else." Alongside his military education, Prince Charles faced another, very particular challenge: the hunt for a suitable wife, with whom he could create his very own home.

Images © Getty, Shutterstock, Topfoto

Charles rehearses at Cambridge

During his days at Cambridge University, Prince Charles was free to indulge his passion for arts and theatre. In addition to his studies and his duties as heir to the throne, he found time to join the famous Footlights Dramatic Club, which birthed dozens of the UK's most celebrated actors, including Olivia Colman, who plays the Prince's mother in series three of *The Crown*. Prince Charles's passion for theatre continues to this day, and he is president of the Royal Shakespeare Company (RSC). In 2016 he even made a guest appearance in a televised comedy sketch for the RSC's *Shakespeare Live!*.

— *1969* —

Princess Margaret and Antony Armstrong-Jones pose after the announcement of their engagement in 1960

LOVE WON AND LOST

Under the ever-watchful eye of the press, one member of the royal family wasn't shy about broken hearts and having fun

Words by **Katharine Marsh**

"I would like it to be known that I have decided not to marry Group Captain Peter Townsend." With a simple sentence, it was all over. Years of stolen moments, furtive glances and falling in love ended in a heartbeat on 31 October 1955. Margaret and her father's equerry had enjoyed a whirlwind relationship - they had come so close to marriage, but the princess would have lost everything.

Instead she let Peter go, but the damage had already been done with the press. While her older sister was the Queen, the epitome of grace and honour, the wilder Margaret, so eager to marry a divorced man, had shown that was prepared to push the boundaries usually obeyed by the royal family, and the papers were ready for whatever came next.

Margaret was quick to recover herself, and she formed what has come to be known as the 'Margaret Set'. Night after night they would attend the theatre, dine at restaurants and stay up until the early hours at nightclubs across London, smoking endless cigarettes and drinking seemingly bottomless tumblers of whisky. The London society scene of the 1950s was theirs,

with illustrious figures like the Marquess of Blandford and Billy Wallace, the son of the minister for transport, forming part of the group.

In the mornings, Margaret wouldn't rise until 11am, when she'd have a pot of weak tea and pick from a plate of fruit. After a bath, she'd be at her desk at around 12.30pm, answering correspondence from friends - she'd always know which letters were theirs thanks to their initials on the bottom left-hand corner of the envelopes.

Lunch was spent with her mother and members of the royal household, and the tensions were clear to see. Margaret was apparently sometimes rude to the Queen Mother, and once asked her, "Why do you dress in those ridiculous clothes?" Later on in the day while watching television, she would also switch to another channel if she wasn't enjoying what her mother was watching. The Queen Mother never said anything to her, though, instead apparently showing her frustration in "the way she moved a book, a piece of furniture or a glass," according to her page William Tallon.

Some have come to the conclusion that Margaret's attitude was down to the fact that she

was always the second-in-line. She was the second child, the youngest, and when her father became king, it was Elizabeth who had received the attention as the heir to the throne. Elizabeth had received an education that Margaret had sorely wanted. Elizabeth was allowed to serve on a Council of State aged just 18, while Margaret had to wait until she was 21. Margaret was trying to rebel, but in doing so she had to walk a fine line between party girl and princess.

But as Margaret's party days made headlines around the world and she stood dutifully with her mother and sister when required, the real question the press wanted answering was who would she marry? Endless rumours swirled around Fleet Street, with close friends and the sons of powerful men considered to be the next in line to propose to the princess. Various names were bandied about - Colin Tennant, Sunny Blandford, Dominic Elliot. Who would finally sweep her off her feet?

In 1956, the world seemed close to getting its answer. Seemingly fed up, a year after the end of her engagement to Townsend, Margaret declared that it was better to marry "somebody one at least

Margaret and Tony pose with their children, David and Sarah

Margaret wasn't just loved by the British press. Here she is on the cover of Italian weekly magazine *Epoca*

liked" than living her life alone at Clarence House. While her mother also resided there, the doors to their suites were on different floors - if it wasn't for their lunches, they could have gone days without seeing each other.

The someone Margaret liked turned out to be Billy Wallace, a member of her inner circle and the son of Euan Wallace, a late former minister of transport who had left him with a small fortune. Unlike the princess's first paramour, he wasn't divorced, he wasn't in the employ of the royal family, and his family was of good standing in society. He was everything the suitor of a queen's sister should be. Margaret said yes when he proposed - why wouldn't she? - and they were sure that they would get Elizabeth's approval. Perhaps this would be Margaret's happy ending after all the heartbreak.

Margaret and Billy's engagement didn't even make it to the newspapers. Before officially asking the Queen for permission, Billy went on holiday to the Bahamas and had a holiday fling. When he returned to London, he told Margaret, thinking that nothing could end their engagement - they were friends, after all. Billy couldn't have misread

the situation more if he'd tried and Margaret quickly broke the relationship off, unwilling to go through with the arrangement if he couldn't at least remain loyal. He would later find love in Elizabeth Hoyer Millar, and they married in 1965 with Margaret in attendance.

But for now, Margaret was alone again. The list of suitors grew, with Margaret being connected to more and more men. We don't know if any of the rumours were grounded in truth - perhaps we never will - but newspapers and tabloids keenly kept up-to-date with the princess's social life. While Elizabeth was demure and regal, Margaret was glamorous and sparkling, every bit the socialite. But for all their theorising and speculating, one man slipped under the radar of every single journalist. Without anyone knowing, he wormed his way into the heart of the poised and stylish princess.

Antony 'Tony' Armstrong-Jones was a photographer, and a very good one at that. His parents - a barrister and a society hostess - had split when he was five, with his mother becoming the Countess of Rosse when she remarried. Tony's childhood has been described as loveless and

Margaret and Tony in the Bahamas in 1967

"THERE WAS MORE TO TONY. HE WAS A REBEL, A BOHEMIAN"

emotionally charged, and that doesn't seem to have been far from the truth. When he contracted polio as a child, he spent six months in hospital and the only family who came to visit him was his sister Susan. His education took him to Eton College and Cambridge University, although he failed his second-year exams in architecture.

It's unclear how Tony and Margaret first met. Some say that Tony had been a royal photographer at Buckingham Palace when they first laid eyes on each other, while others claim that the pair met at a dinner party in Chelsea in 1958. The princess was apparently drawn in by his impish smile and his sense of mischief - he seemed to complement Margaret. And for a royal who wanted to rebel, Tony seemed like the perfect choice; here was a man who could show her a

whole new world, and her family viewed him as nothing but a 'humble tradesman' because of his profession. Anything to wind them up was a plus.

But there was more to Tony. He himself was a rebel, a bohemian living through the 1950s, before the sexual revolution gripped the world. At first Margaret hadn't even considered him a potential match, instead thinking that he was gay, but she wasn't actually that far from the truth. It has become well known that Tony was bisexual, and it was in a time when homosexuality was considered illegal in the United Kingdom.

In the late 1950s, Tony's libido never seemed to be satisfied. While he began to romance Margaret, men and women would frequent his studio, and not all of them were visiting solely for photography. Affairs were carried out with Jacqui

Colin Tennant
An Old Etonian, Colin was the son of the second Baron Glenconner. There was much speculation that he was in a relationship with Margaret, which he later downplayed by claiming, "I don't expect she would have had me."

Sunny Blandford
Part of the Spencer-Churchill family and heir to the duchy of Marlborough, Sunny (nicknamed for his courtesy title of Earl of Sunderland was considered one of the most likely to marry Princess Margaret.

Billy Wallace
Briefly engaged to the princess, Billy was the grandson of architect Sir Edwin Lutyens. Educated at Eton and Oxford, he later married the Hon. Elizabeth Millar. He died just a few days before his fiftieth birthday.

Dominic Elliot
The son of the Earl of Minto, Dominic spent many an evening in London with Margaret. Despite rumours of a relationship with the princess, he went on to marry twice, in 1962 and later 1983.

Mark Bonham Carter
Son of Liberal activists and a member of the prominent Bonham Carter family, Mark was part of the Margaret Set before his marriage in 1955 to Leslie, Lady St Just. He died in 1994.

Chan, a dancer who is often considered to have been Tony's first real girlfriend, and Gina Ward, an actress. But that wasn't where the relationships stopped. It's difficult to prove, but some have suggested that Tony was part of a scandalous open relationship with two of his married friends, Jeremy and Camilla Fry.

It's unclear how much of this Margaret knew at the time. Was she aware that in the same terrace house in Bermondsey where she was perhaps falling in love, Tony was sleeping with other women? That he was conducting affairs right up until 1959? He was incredibly secretive, so it's likely that the princess didn't have an inkling.

Margaret was enthralled, enraptured by this bohemian man who didn't shy away from her. When taking her portraits, he was able to get her to change her clothes, her position - no one had ever really managed to tell her what to do before. He oozed charisma, and he was a challenge. Margaret had never really had a challenge before; it was new, exciting.

Then in October 1959, while the couple were visiting Balmoral Castle, a letter arrived. It was from Townsend, and it could have been better news - he was announcing his engagement. The bride-to-be was Marie-Luce Jamagne, a 19-year-old Belgian who bore a striking resemblance to the princess. The press would have a field day. But Margaret wanted to prove that she was over him, that she had left their relationship behind and moved on. She encouraged Tony not to propose so that there could be no reports of her being desperate or wanting to get one up on her ex-fiancé and his new flame.

But a proposal was coming. Over Christmas that year, Tony asked for the Queen's permission, and Elizabeth was eager to give it and to see her sister happy. The ring, a large ruby, cost £250 and had been designed by Tony himself to look like a rosebud. When Tony gave it to the princess, she was delighted. She said yes.

As always with Margaret, problems weren't far away. When she was ready to officially announce

Margaret often headed to her villa in Mustique to spend time away from her husband

"AS ALWAYS WITH MARGARET, PROBLEMS WEREN'T FAR AWAY"

the engagement in February 1960, she had to wait - her sister, the Queen, the one who always came first, had given birth to Prince Andrew on the 19th, and the betrothal couldn't be made public for fear of upstaging her. Finally, on 26 February, Margaret got her moment. She told the world she was getting married, and the big day was 6 May.

The media and the country were shocked - no one had seen this coming. At every party, every public event, Tony had managed to fade into the background. No journalist had so much as glanced his way; he wasn't an eligible bachelor, and certainly not a man who would catch the eye of the Queen's sister. And there hadn't even been any mention of the couple being romantically involved before the announcement.

Congratulations flew in from around the world, but hidden among them were warnings. Lady Elizabeth Cavendish told Margaret, "You won't always know where he is and he won't always

WORKING FOR MARGARET

What was it really like to serve the princess?

Being in the employ of the royal family was something one aimed for – especially being a member of the household staff of the monarch or one of her close relatives. People relished the chance to work for the Queen and the Queen Mother, and even Princess Margaret, although at times it's hard to see why.

Margaret could be notoriously unfair to her staff. Each year, Buckingham Palace held a Christmas party that the staff of Clarence House were invited to, and the Queen Mother would either dine out or have a light meal so that her household

could go and join the fun. Her younger daughter, on the other hand, would hold a dinner party, keeping her staff on the clock. When at lunch with her mother, she would also be rude and dismissive to her mother's household staff.

One royal servant, Peter Russel, who served the royal family from 1954 to 1968, claims that at banquets someone would have to stand next to Margaret holding an ashtray "so she didn't have to look to see where she flicked her ash". Working for Margaret wasn't necessarily the dream job everyone thought it was.

Clarence House, home to Princess Margaret before her marriage

It may have looked like a fairytale, but the magic wasn't to last, as Margaret and Tony's relationship devolved into affairs, recriminations and divorce

ISSUED UNDER THE AUTHORITY OF THE MINISTER OF WORKS

THE MARRIAGE OF HER ROYAL HIGHNESS
PRINCESS MARGARET
WITH
MR ANTONY ARMSTRONG-JONES
FRIDAY 6 MAY 1960 · HORSE GUARDS PARADE

ADMIT ONE | BLOCK M | ROW C | SEAT 13

A ticket to the wedding procession of Margaret and Tony

want to tell you." Lord de Vesci, Tony's brother-in-law, meanwhile, bluntly said, "Tony, for God's sake, don't." None of the advice was heeded. Tony had already broken off his other affairs, and he was now all Margaret's.

When 6 May came around, no expense had been spared. The ceremony was the first British royal wedding to be broadcast on television, and 300 million people tuned in around the world. It had to be decadent, like something out of a fairy tale, and Margaret made sure that it was, to the cost of £86,000. 2,000 guests waited in Westminster Abbey, and they included Winston Churchill, European royalty, and some of the leading film stars of the 1950s.

Her dress was made from silk organza and designed by Norman Hartnell, who had created Elizabeth's wedding gown in 1947. The skirt alone was made of 30 metres of fabric, and she parted with tradition by wearing the Poltimore tiara rather than a headpiece from the Crown Jewel collection. She was always going to have something different - something that showed she'd stamped her own mark on the day.

After making the journey to the Abbey from Clarence House in the Glass Coach, Margaret walked the aisle with her brother-in-law, the Duke of Edinburgh, to meet her soon-to-be husband at the altar. There he stood, alongside his best man - but Roger Gilliat

hadn't been his first choice. The position had belonged to Jeremy Fry until it was revealed that he had a criminal conviction from 1952 as a result of 'homosexual acts'. It simply wouldn't do to have scandal at the wedding, so he was replaced. The wedding breakfast was at Buckingham Palace, and the newlyweds stepped out onto the balcony to greet the well wishers who lined the Mall. Inside the palace were 20 wedding cakes and a 60-foot floral arch - no expense had been spared. And married life seemed to suit the couple. Their six-week honeymoon was spent on the Royal Yacht Britannia, and they returned to live at Kensington Palace. Later that year they became the Earl and Countess of Snowdon, and Tony took the title of Viscount Linley; the 1960s were off to a great start for both of them. But soon after the happy couple had tied the knot, Camilla Fry gave birth to a baby girl. While she was married, her claim was that Jeremy wasn't the child's father - according to her, it was Tony. Camilla never went public with her claim, and the girl, Polly, was raised believing that Jeremy was her father. Tony didn't take a DNA test until 2004, when his paternity was confirmed. As always with the royals, it's unclear how much the royal family knew about this.

Life was different for the married couple. Tony had to switch his jeans and leather jackets for well-cut suits, and he was made to switch to British cigarettes. But one thing he wouldn't change was his career – photography was his passion, and he wasn't going to let it go. On 23 January 1961, he joined the Council of Industrial Design as an unpaid designer, and more good news was on the way: Margaret was pregnant. David Albert Charles was born on 3 November, and he was christened in December at Buckingham Palace. One child turned into two when the countess gave birth to a girl, Sarah Frances Elizabeth, on 1 May 1964.

All the while, Apartment 1A, Kensington Palace, was turning into a society hotspot. An invitation to a party or dinner there was highly sought after in an age where any invitation to royal events was rare. Britain's most glamorous couple played host to the era's most celebrated musicians, actors and poets, and Margaret would often play the piano and sing her favourite musical tracks to entertain her guests.

But the wedded bliss wouldn't last forever. As the 1960s progressed, cracks started to appear in their marriage. Tony was becoming ever more immersed in his work, travelling around Britain and abroad. He was seen escorting young, attractive models, and Margaret was beginning to get jealous. She became possessive, phoning him to find out his whereabouts or appearing at his studio. When Tony came home, he would lock himself in his basement workroom and refuse his wife's insistences that he meet guests.

As time wore on, he started to become outright cruel. When attending a party on the private island of Spetsopoula, he told Margaret to wear a ball gown when everyone else was wearing jeans and sandals, and he brought presents for everyone except his wife. He would belittle her in front of their friends, and he left nasty notes between the pages of her books, with one apparently reading,

The Earl and Countess of Snowdon were every inch the country's most glamorous couple, paving the way for royalty today. Here they are photographed with Elton John in 1972

"HE BROUGHT PRESENTS FOR EVERYONE EXCEPT HIS WIFE"

"You look like a Jewish manicurist and I hate you." Arguments became more common. Margaret began spending time away at her villa on Mustique, which had been given to her as a wedding present. Tony was having a string of extramarital affairs and his wife was left wondering what went wrong. She'd married him out of an act of rebellion – he wasn't a royal, he was a commoner – but it hadn't turned out as she'd hoped. She was alone, attending functions by herself as Tony travelled the world.

By the late 1970s, the marriage was falling apart. Divorce seemed to be off the table – Princess Margaret was the sister of the Queen, after all – but it was clear that Margaret and Tony weren't happy. It only got worse when Margaret took Roddy Llewllyn, who was 17 years younger than her, to Mustique in 1976. It was a national scandal; the

tabloids had a field day, finding every angle on the story of the beautiful, troubled princess and a younger man who wasn't her husband holidaying in the West Indies together.

There was only one course of action left open to Tony and Margaret: they announced their separation. Tony apparently told Margaret's personal secretary that he was done, using the scandal as his excuse to get out. When she was told, Margaret is said to have replied, "Oh, I see. Thank you... I think that's the best news you've ever given me."

But there was one more scandal for Margaret. Finally, after two years of separation, the announcement was issued on 10 May 1978: "Her Royal Highness The Princess Margaret, Countess of Snowdon, and the Earl of Snowdon, after two years of separation, have agreed that their marriage should be formally ended."

It was over. For the first time in 77 years, a senior royal was divorcing their partner. Margaret's reputation had been cemented, and, as she would later say herself, "It was inevitable, when there are two sisters and one is the Queen, who must be the source of honour and all that is good, while the other must be the focus of the most creative malice, the evil sister."

Throughout their marriage, Tony was often pictured with young, attractive models, fuelling speculation that he was being unfaithful

Jacqui Chan, Tony's long-term lover right up until the announcement of his engagement to Margaret

A PRINCESS OF THE ARTS

Uncover Margaret's love for art, dance and fashion

For someone brought up in the strict world of royal protocol, where not a hair can be out of place, art can be a refuge. Paintings and sculptures can express things in ways that words can't, and that can draw in a viewer that's looking for creativity in a world full of stiffness.

Perhaps this was why Margaret loved art so much. She could often be found at museums and galleries, and it's little wonder that she fell in love with a photographer. In fact, Margaret was fascinated by the new world she discovered through Tony. There were actors, journalists, painters and poets, all with more stories to tell than the last and with powerful personalities to boot. Here was the vibrancy that she had been looking for her whole life.

One of Margaret's greatest loves was ballet, and she became the first president of the Royal Ballet in 1957, but she would always be known as the most fashionable royal of her era. With a love for the extravagant, it was a way for her to express her station above others in one of the only ways she could while always having to remain one step behind her elder sister.

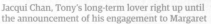

Princess Margaret often went out in London surrounded by male friends

Princess Margaret said of Picasso's *Woman's Head*, "Like it, loathe it, but admit... it's eye-catching"

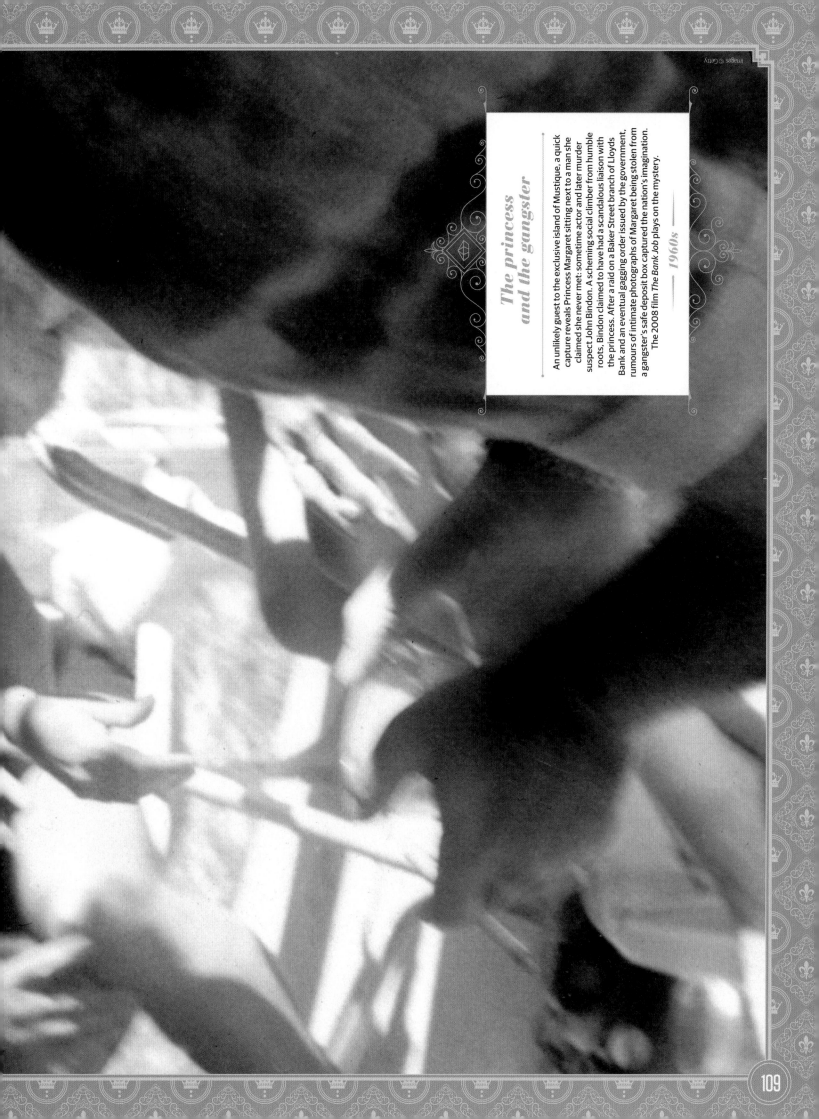

The princess and the gangster

An unlikely guest to the exclusive island of Mustique, a quick capture reveals Princess Margaret sitting next to a man she claimed she never met: sometime actor and later murder suspect John Bindon. A scheming social climber from humble roots, Bindon claimed to have had a scandalous liaison with the princess. After a raid on a Baker Street branch of Lloyds Bank and an eventual gagging order issued by the government, rumours of intimate photographs of Margaret being stolen from a gangster's safe deposit box captured the nation's imagination. The 2008 film *The Bank Job* plays on the mystery.

— *1960s* —

The Queen allowed cameramen
unprecedented access to her family's
private life while they filmed *Royal Family*
documentary. Here, they are being filmed
having breakfast at Windsor Castle

AN ERA OF TURBULENCE

As Britain faced a period of great change, the 1960s and 1970s were challenging decades for the Queen and her family

Words by **Melanie Clegg** & **Jessica Leggett**

Between 1964 and 1976, many social and cultural changes were taking place in Britain as the Swinging Sixties got underway, Beatlemania dominated the headlines and Harold Wilson led the first Labour government since the 1940s. It was an exciting and eventful time for everyone - including the royal family.

When Queen Elizabeth gave birth to her fourth and final child, Prince Edward, on 10 March 1964, she was absolutely delighted with her new baby. "Goodness, what fun it is to have a baby in the house again!" she exclaimed, relishing the prospect of enjoying a more relaxed relationship with her two youngest children. When her eldest two children, Charles and Anne, were born, the Queen was in her early 20s and had not expected to inherit the throne for several more decades. By the time of Prince Edward's birth, however, much had changed: she was just a month shy of her 38th birthday and had been on the throne for over a decade. She was no longer the shy and rather awkward young princess who had so disliked public displays of affection and felt as though her onerous royal duties struck a poor

balance with her other duties as a wife and mother. Instead, she was now a confident, mature woman who was more than ready and able to rise to the challenge of being both a mother and a monarch. However, although the Queen was happy to have another baby, her duties quickly took her elsewhere. She agreed to go on a ten-day tour of Canada at the end of the year - it was a disaster, marred by an assassination threat, booing in Quebec City and a riot in Montréal, all of which challenged her famous sang-froid, and she no doubt wished she had stayed at home instead.

Over the next decade, the royal family would see many other challenges as the world changed and the elder royal children matured and started their own independent lives, with plenty of mishaps and dramas along the way. It was also a period of great personal satisfaction for the Queen as she worked hard to boost the royal family's popularity. She made them more visible by authorising a groundbreaking documentary and also introducing walkabouts to her royal engagements, which allowed her to meet more members of the public. She also enjoyed working with her first Labour prime minister, Harold

Wilson, who was elected in October 1964 and stayed in power until June 1970, when he was ousted by the Conservative Edward Heath. Unlike the well-heeled privately educated men who had been her previous prime ministers, Harold Wilson was of proudly provincial stock and had attended a grammar school before going to Oxford, where he excelled in Economics. If the Queen had felt nervous about dealing with a noted socialist, she need not have worried. She and Wilson became great friends and thoroughly enjoyed their weekly meetings, which often went well over the allotted time as they had so much to talk about.

Within just a few weeks of Prince Edward's birth, the inner circle of the royal household was shaken by the revelation that the Surveyor of the Queen's Pictures, the eminent art historian Sir Anthony Blunt (who was a distant cousin of the Queen Mother) had confessed to acting as a Soviet spy. He had been recruited by Guy Burgess in the 1930s, and was in fact the hitherto mysterious 'Fourth Man' of the notorious Cambridge Spy Ring, made up of intellectual Communists. Although there had been rumours about Blunt's involvement in espionage for several years, the

The Queen was deeply moved, often to tears, by the sights that she saw when she visited Aberfan shortly after the disaster in October 1966

revelation came as a huge shock to the Queen, who had no idea. In exchange for his confession, Blunt was offered immunity from prosecution and for his secret to be embargoed for 15 years, which meant that he was able to continue in his post as usual. However, after his secret was revealed in 1979, his life was effectively ruined. He was forced to resign his post in the royal household and was stripped of the knighthood that had been awarded to him in 1956. After he died of a heart attack in 1983, Blunt's memoirs revealed that he believed that becoming a spy had been "the biggest mistake" of his life.

A very different sort of drama was brewing elsewhere in the royal household as the marriage of the Queen's younger sister, Princess Margaret, to photographer Lord Snowdon became increasingly unhappy. The birth of the couple's second child in May 1964 brought them together for a time, but things quickly began to unravel between them against a vivid backdrop of glamorous celebrity parties, expensive overseas holidays and possible alcohol and drug abuse.

"1966 WOULD BE A YEAR BOTH OF TRIUMPH AND TRAGEDY THAT UNITED THE NATION"

While her elder sister felt distinctly uncomfortable in celebrity circles, Margaret loved to surround herself with bohemians - The Beatles and The Rolling Stones dominated headlines, and she was happy to absorb them into her social circle.

In November 1965, Queen Elizabeth made a bold decision to send Princess Margaret and Lord Snowdon on a three-week overseas tour to the United States. At the time, relations between Britain and the US were deteriorating, as was the relationship between Wilson and President Lyndon B Johnson. Britain was in serious debt, the economy was in trouble and the country needed a loan from the International Monetary Fund, which could only be granted with the US's approval. Also

Britain, in the middle of decolonisation, did not support the US involvement in the Vietnam War, which strained relations further. It was hoped that the princess's visit would help smooth things over.

Margaret and her husband arrived in California, travelling to San Francisco, Los Angeles and Arizona, partying with Hollywood stars such as Judy Garland, Frank Sinatra, Elizabeth Taylor, and Richard Burton along the way. Upon their arrival in Washington, DC, Johnson hosted a formal dinner at the White House to celebrate their visit, with the party afterwards lasting until 1.40am. While Margaret and Lord Snowdon were a success in the US, their late-night antics, the wild behaviour of their entourage, and the cost of the

The Aberfan disaster of 1966 shocked the nation

It was the family's most sensational event of the era, so why did Netflix overlook the botched abduction of Anne?

On the night of 20 March 1974 – barely five months after celebrating the high of their wedding with the nation – Princess Anne and her husband experienced a very terrifying kind of low that occasionally comes with living under the public eye. Travelling back to Buckingham Palace after a royal engagement, the couple – joined by their protection officer James Beaton, Anne's lady-in-waiting Rowena Brassey, as well as their chauffeur Alex Callender – almost became victims of a kidnapping plot. As the royal vehicle drove down the Mall, a car swerved in front, forcing the royals to stop. The car's driver, Ian Ball, stepped out, brandishing two handguns.

As Beaton jumped into action, he was quickly shot in the shoulder, as was Callender when he attempted to disarm Ball. While Ball advanced on Princess Anne, demanding that she come with him ("Not bloody likely," she famously retorted), several passers-by, including journalist Brian McConnell and former boxer Ron Russell, intervened before Police Constable Michael Hills stumbled across the scene and called for back-up. For his efforts, Hills was shot, but not before his request was answered. Detective Constable Peter Edmonds responded pursued Ball, before arresting him. He pleaded guilty to attempted murder and kidnapping. All those shot recovered, while Ball was committed to Broadmoor Hospital.

The story made newspaper headlines and saw Anne praised for her cool demeanour in the face of danger. In arguably the family's most mundane decade, then, it seems incredible that the writers of *The Crown* chose to overlook this larger-than-life event, instead exaggerating other storylines to almost-fictional proportions, including the alleged involvement of Lord Mountbatten in a coup against Harold Wilson.

trip – an eye-watering £30,000 – caused a negative reaction back in Britain. When the couple wanted to return for another tour in the 1970s, they were banned from doing so by British diplomats.

Although her husband had been unfaithful throughout their marriage, Margaret reportedly did not have her first affair until around 1966 when she began a liaison with Anthony Barton, a friend of the Snowdons and godfather to their daughter. She had a number of discreet affairs until she met Roderic 'Roddy' Llewellyn, who was 17 years her junior, in 1973. Although Margaret described their relationship as a "loving friendship", it's clear that she was devoted to him. When photos of the pair on holiday together appeared on the front page of *The News of the World*, it was the catalyst for the final breakdown and end of her marriage, which resulted in a divorce in July 1978. Lord Snowdon swiftly married again, but Margaret would remain unmarried for the rest of her life.

The nation mourned when news broke on 21 October 1966 about the terrible tragedy that had befallen the small Welsh mining village of Aberfan. One of the enormous colliery spoil tips, precariously balanced on a hillside above the village, collapsed and descended upon the village in a horrifying avalanche of slurry, almost completely burying the Pantglas Junior School. There were 144 deaths, including those of 116 children, most of them pupils at the school.

Early the next morning, Lord Snowdon visited the site and spoke to parents of victims and rescue workers while his brother-in-law, the Duke of Edinburgh, arrived a few hours later. However, the Queen did not visit until the following week, a delay that she would later describe as one of her biggest regrets. She would ultimately visit the village four more times over the years and the people of Aberfan still believe that her continued interest in them has done a great deal to help them recover from the disaster. It reminded them that they had not been forgotten by the world.

The 1960s are remembered as an era of great social and cultural change. The younger generation, who had been born immediately after

Unlike her sister, Princess Margaret felt very much at home with celebrities and was clearly delighted to meet The Beatles at a film premiere in July 1964

The Crown faithfully re-created the emotional scenes in the wake of the Aberfan disaster of October 1966

Ian Ball, Princess Anne's would-be kidnapper, is led in handcuffs from a police van to court, where he was charged with attempted murder and kidnapping

the war and now benefited from the new prosperity that had succeeded post-war austerity, celebrated all that was fresh, modern and innovative. In the eyes of many, the royal family epitomised the dull and old-fashioned past that they were trying their utmost to distance themselves from. It was time for the royals to reflect on their place in this new world and consider ways to make themselves appear more relevant and approachable.

In early 1968, the Queen decided to authorise a groundbreaking documentary about her family. Ostensibly it was to celebrate the investiture of Prince Charles as Prince of Wales the following year, but it would also make the family appear more accessible and less remote. Over the next year, cameramen were allowed unprecedented access to the Queen and her family (with one notable absentee - the Duke of Edinburgh's mother, Alice, who had moved into Buckingham Palace in 1967) as they went about their daily business. The filmmakers accumulated 43 hours of footage, which was condensed into an 110-minute documentary, titled *Royal Family*.

However, when it was screened in June 1969, with more than 30 million curious British viewers tuning in, the response was decidedly muted. Many critics thought that presenting the Queen and her family as ordinary people destroyed some of the intrinsic mystique of royalty, and that in the long term it would do them more harm than good. It was therefore decided that the film should be shelved and never again be broadcast in public.

When Prince Charles's investiture, a medieval modern spectacle devised by Lord Snowdon, took place a few weeks later, it too was marred by controversy. Although the majority of Welsh people were in favour of the ceremony, a significant proportion - many of whom were members of Welsh nationalist and republican groups - made their disapproval known and even threatened to disrupt the event at Caernarfon Castle. Even the news that Prince Charles had spent several months learning about Welsh culture and had even been studying the Welsh language for the event, did little to improve matters, although in the end the ceremony passed without incident.

While the royal family were preparing for the investiture, preparations of a very different kind were underway elsewhere as NASA got ready for one of the most exciting and highly anticipated events of the 20th century - the first manned Moon landing. The royal family were amongst the 650 million viewers worldwide who watched Neil Armstrong and Buzz Aldrin descend from Apollo 11's lunar lander on 20 July 1969, becoming the first men to walk on the Moon. It was a thrilling moment, and perhaps few were quite so excited as the Duke of Edinburgh, who was deeply interested in the possibilities of extraterrestrial life and UFOs, even keeping a map of alleged sightings on a wall in Buckingham Palace. To actually see men walking on the Moon would have been absolutely

Prince Charles's investiture as Prince of Wales caused some controversy amongst Welsh nationalists and republicans, but despite threats to disrupt the event it was considered a great success

fascinating for a man with his interests. Meanwhile, his wife was also enthralled by the mission and deeply impressed by the bravery of the astronauts. "I salute the skills and courage which have brought man to the Moon," she wrote to them. "May this endeavour increase the knowledge and well being of mankind." She and Prince Philip were both delighted to meet the Apollo 11 crew when they attended a reception at Buckingham Palace later that year. Afterwards, Armstrong and Aldrin commented on how amazingly well informed and interested about their programme the Queen had been.

Prince Charles met the vivacious Camilla Shand in 1971 but the couple split up when he started his RAF training and she married someone else

When Princess Anne turned 20 in August 1970, it meant that both of the Queen's eldest children were now officially out of their teens. Prince Charles graduated from the University of Cambridge that summer, then began training with the RAF before emulating his father and grandfather by embarking on a career in the Royal Navy. In 1971, shortly after beginning his training, he met vivacious socialite Camilla Shand, with whom he was immediately smitten. Although it would turn out that she was more interested in his sister Anne's ex-boyfriend, a dashing Household Cavalry officer called Andrew Parker Bowles, whom Camilla would eventually marry.

While her brother was starting his career, Princess Anne was concentrating on her passion for equestrian sports. She won the European Eventing Championships in 1971, which led to her being voted BBC Sports Personality of the Year a few months later. After breaking up with Andrew Parker-Bowles, she married noted equestrian Lieutenant Mark Phillips on 13 November 1973.

However much the newly married couple clearly wanted to enjoy an private and ordinary existence, they were soon reminded just how difficult that would be. Within five months of their wedding, in March 1974 they only narrowly avoided being kidnapped while driving down the

Despite her initial reservations, the Queen and her first Labour prime minister, Harold Wilson, developed an excellent professional relationship and became good friends

Despite the happy facade, Princess Margaret and Lord Snowdon's relationship was crumbling, with the latter leaving the former nasty notes in her books

Queen Elizabeth II with the Apollo 11 astronauts, Michael Collins, Neil Armstrong and Buzz Aldrin, when she met them at Buckingham Palace

Mall. The assailant, Ian Ball, had forced their car to stop then shot Anne's chauffeur and protection officer as well as a journalist who attempted to intervene before demanding that the princess get out of her car. "Not bloody likely!" Anne retorted before making her escape. Ball then shot a police officer before finally being overpowered and arrested. The incident shocked the nation but luckily all those who were shot by Ball recovered from their injuries, while Princess Anne's calm composure and bravery were much admired and won her many new fans.

While Princess Anne's wedding in 1973 was the great royal celebration of the decade, there was another much sadder event in June of the previous year when the Queen's uncle, the Duke of Windsor, was quietly laid to rest in the Royal Burial Ground at Frogmore House after lying in state in St George's Chapel, Windsor Castle. The Duke, whose health had been failing for a number of years, had died in Paris on 28 May, just ten days after the Queen paid him a private visit while on a state visit to the French capital. The Duchess of Windsor accompanied her husband's body to England and stayed at Buckingham Palace, where it was noted that the Queen treated her with great kindness, probably prompted by the fact that the frail Duchess was confused and disorientated and eventually had to be sedated on the day of the funeral. The Queen, as one observer noted later, "showed a motherly and nanny-like tenderness

and kept putting her hand on the Duchess's arm and glove." Edward's abdication and subsequent behaviour over the years had done much to alienate him from his family as well as make him deeply unpopular with the British populace, but by the early 1970s it was clear that the Queen at least was ready to put it all firmly behind her. The Duchess of Windsor developed dementia and lived as a virtual recluse for the last years of her life. When she died in April 1986, she was also accorded a funeral in St George's Chapel and then, in the presence of the Queen and Duke of Edinburgh as well as other members of the royal family, buried beside her husband.

In 1977, the Queen celebrated her Silver Jubilee, marking 25 years since her accession to the throne of the United Kingdom as well as the thrones of other Commonwealth realms. The year-long festivities began on 6 February, the day that the Queen's beloved father, King George VI, passed away and she took the throne, with the Queen posing for a portrait in the Throne Room at Buckingham Palace. She then embarked on a tour with Prince Philip around the Commonwealth and throughout the UK. In June, the Queen went on a procession through London to coincide with her official birthday, with an estimated one million people lining the streets to watch, while another 500 million people watched it live on television.

As for politics, the Queen was no doubt pleased when Harold Wilson was returned to power in

March 1974, after the tumultuous premiership of Edward Heath. During Heath's time as prime minister, there was widespread unrest with miners' strikes in 1972 and 1974 triggering power blackouts across the country, leading to the notorious three-day working week in an attempt to conserve electricity. Heath subsequently lost in the snap general election to Wilson and the following year, he was ousted as leader of the Conservatives.

The Queen had established a remarkable rapport and genuine friendship with Prime Minister Wilson, and the pair were able to resume the weekly meetings that she had enjoyed so much. However, despite all of his socialist government's achievements when it came to making Britain a healthier, safer and fairer place to live, his period in office was a deeply stressful one. He dealt with the decolonisation of the former empire and, closer to home, the increasing threat of militant groups in Northern Ireland. In March 1976, Wilson announced his resignation and as a mark of her respect, the Queen marked his departure by attending a dinner at 10 Downing Street - an honour that had only once before been accorded, to Winston Churchill. Although the Queen was sorry to lose Harold Wilson, she also enjoyed dealing with his successor James Callaghan, who would remain in power until he was replaced in 1979 by Margaret Thatcher - which began an altogether different relationship between the Queen and her prime minister.

A DECADE OF HIGHS & LOWS

Life for the Queen, her family and the British people changed enormously during the 1980s

Words by **Jessica Leggett**

History was made when Margaret Thatcher, leader of the Conservative Party, was elected Britain's first female prime minister on 4 May 1979, securing 43.9 per cent of the votes. Over the next 11 years, her premiership ushered in Thatcherism, the collective term used for her policies and branch of Conservative ideology, which marked the end of the post-war political consensus in Britain and undeniably shaped the nation.

Just three months after Thatcher's win, the royal family was left devastated when the Queen's cousin, Lord Louis Mountbatten, one of his teenage grandsons and two others were killed by an IRA bomb planted on his fishing boat in County Sligo, Ireland. He received a ceremonial funeral at Westminster Abbey on 5 September. Lord Mountbatten had been close to his grand-nephew, Prince Charles, and acted as a mentor and 'honorary grandfather.' He had counselled Charles on many things including his love life, famously encouraging the prince to sow his wild oats, before settling down with a young and inexperienced girl who would be suitable as a future queen. A year after Mountbatten's death, Charles became re-acquainted with Lady Diana Spencer.

Diana was 16 when she met Charles – who was almost 13 years her senior – for the first time in November 1977, during a grouse hunt at the Spencer family home, Althorp. They had been introduced by her oldest sister, Sarah, who briefly dated Charles at the time. When they met again in 1980, Diana was sympathetic towards Charles, who was still grieving the loss of his mentor and she later recalled their conversation: "We were talking about Mountbatten and his girlfriend and I said, 'You must be so lonely.' I said, 'It's pathetic watching you walking up the aisle with Mountbatten's coffin in front, ghastly, you need someone beside you.'"

It was after this that Charles began to consider Diana as a potential bride and they subsequently began courting, largely through phone calls. Charles invited her to join him on the royal yacht, HMY Britannia, followed by an invitation to meet his family, notably the Queen, the Duke of Edinburgh and the Queen Mother, at their Scottish residence Balmoral in November 1980.

If Diana aced the so-called Balmoral Test, Mrs Thatcher was not so fortunate. Lady Diana Spencer had spent her early childhood on the Sandringham Estate, where she could count the royal children as playmates. However, Thatcher and Queen Elizabeth II were from different worlds. The prime minister, steeped in the world of Westminster, found herself a fish out of water during the visits to Balmoral that were seemingly so effortless for Diana when she visited Charles.

By now, the press had cottoned on to the burgeoning relationship between Diana and the prince, which led to intense media scrutiny regarding a possible marriage. Concerned about the constant speculation and Charles's indecision, Philip encouraged his son to hurry up and decide whether he wanted to propose – both for his sake and Diana's reputation. Under pressure from his family and the press, Charles turned to Camilla Parker Bowles for guidance. When she encouraged him to move on and make something of his new relationship, the Prince of Wales capitulated. Charles got down on one knee and proposed with a sapphire and diamond engagement ring during a private dinner at Buckingham Palace, with Diana accepting immediately.

The couple announced their engagement three weeks later on 24 February 1981. They had an interview with the BBC that day at the Palace, with Charles stating that he was "delighted and frankly amazed that Diana is prepared to take me on," whilst Diana shyly admitted that she was "delighted and thrilled, blissfully happy." However, the cracks in their relationship were already

Charles and Diana ride in a
carriage after their wedding
at St Paul's Cathedral

starting to show - when the couple was asked if they were in love, Charles infamously responded with "whatever 'in love' means." Diana later admitted that his answer "traumatised" her. As she submitted to lessons in how a princess should behave, Diana became increasingly concerned about Charles's relationship with Camilla and her own shaky relationship with her fiancé. After the two women met for lunch, Diana seriously considered calling off the wedding but pushed her concerns aside, desperate to make her marriage work.

On 29 July that year, Charles and Diana were married at St Paul's Cathedral, London, in a televised ceremony that was seen by around 150 million people around the globe. The bride's iconic wedding dress was made from an ivory silk taffeta and antique lace gown with a 25-foot train, designed by David and Elizabeth Emanuel. With her marriage to Charles, Diana became the first Englishwoman to marry the heir to the throne in three centuries - the last one was Anne Hyde, who had married the future King James II in 1660.

Aside from the wedding, 1981 was a busy year in general for the royal family. In May, Princess Anne gave birth to her daughter and the Queen's first granddaughter, Zara. Zara was Anne's second child with her husband, Captain Mark Phillips, as their first son and the Queen's first grandchild, Peter, had been born in 1977.

As the new Prince and Princess of Wales embarked on their unhappy marriage, the so-called Iron Lady crumbled. When her son, Mark, disappeared whilst competing in the Paris-Dakar Rally, Thatcher's icy calm demeanour melted. Though Mark was found safe and well, the Queen's own family was far from happy thanks to the deterioration of the marriage of Diana and Charles, who continued to seek solace in Camilla.

Emma Corrin stars as Princess Diana in the fourth series

The Queen and Thatcher may have clashed at times, but they respected one another

The year after the royal family celebrated the wedding of the Prince and Princess of Wales, the Queen found herself at the centre of a rather less happy occasion. At 7am on 9 July 1982, a man named Michael Fagan scaled the wall of Buckingham Palace, climbed up a drainpipe and entered the royal residence. As he wandered around the building towards the royal apartments, he triggered the security alarm twice but it was turned off by the police, who believed that it was faulty. Around 15 minutes after breaking into the Palace, Fagan entered the Queen's bedroom and pulled back a curtain, waking her up. Reports at the time claimed that he had sat at the end of the Queen's bed, but Fagan later admitted that she had left the room immediately to call security and that police had failed to arrive, despite being called twice. In the end, he was finally arrested after Paul Whybrew, a footman, arrived with two policemen, although he was ultimately not charged for trespassing. The incident has since been widely described as one of the worst royal security breaches of the 20th century.

Meanwhile, less than three weeks before the break-in, the nation was elated when Diana gave birth to Prince William Arthur Philip Louis at St Mary's Hospital, Paddington, London, on 21 June 1982. As the firstborn son of Charles and Diana, he was second in line to the British throne after his father, and he was also the first child to be born to a prince and princess of Wales in 77 years.

While the royal family had a busy start to the 1980s, Margaret Thatcher had also had her hands full during her first term as prime minister. In the mid-1970s, inflation had risen to over 25% and it was Thatcher's job to try and tame it, which she did with a series of liberalising economic policies, including a sharp increase in interest rates.

However, the United Kingdom subsequently entered a recession, which left 2 million people unemployed by the autumn of 1980. In October, Thatcher famously responded to those who wanted her to do a U-turn on her policies, stating that "The lady's not for turning," during her speech at the Conservative Party conference.

Thatcher also had to deal with the rising tensions between the United Kingdom and Argentina over the Falkland Islands, located in the South Atlantic. Argentina had claimed sovereignty over the Falklands, a British overseas territory, for

years, and on 2 April 1982, the Argentinians invaded the Falklands. Thatcher responded by sending a naval task force, including the Royal Navy and the Royal Fleet Auxiliary, to take back the islands. The undeclared war between the two nations lasted for a total of 74 days with a series of engagements, which left three Falklands civilians, 255 British troops and around 650 Argentinians dead. It ended with Argentina's surrender on 14 June, thereby restoring British control over the Falkland Islands.

The Queen riding sidesaddle during the Trooping the Colour procession, 1981

The quick victory helped to secure a desperately needed surge in popularity for Thatcher, who was consequently re-elected for a second term by a landslide in June 1983, securing a huge majority of 144 seats. With this majority, Thatcher and the Conservatives were able to usher in tax cuts, privatisation, deregulation and trade union reform.

Undeterred by her critics, Thatcher continued to push through her policies, which included privatising major utilities such as British Telecom, British Aerospace and British Gas, alongside organisations like British Airways and Rolls-Royce. In fact, during her 11 years as prime minister, over 40 previously state-owned businesses in the UK had been privatised.

While Thatcher was taking on the miners and privatising national industries, Diana had given birth to her second son, Prince Henry Charles Albert David, on 15 September 1984 at St Mary's Hospital. Affectionately known as Harry, the new prince was third in line for the throne at the time of his birth.

When it came to raising her boys, Diana was determined to give her sons a wider upbringing than the one traditionally given to royal children. Diana broke with royal tradition when she insisted that William join her and Charles on their tour of Australia and New Zealand in 1983 – she did the same again two years later by bringing both of their boys on a tour of Italy.

Charles and Diana's trip to Australia was a sensation. Her popularity eclipsed that of Charles and republican fever evaporated in the face of her relatable, disarming presence. Yet even as the Princess of Wales charmed the people and politicians alike, in private Diana was in crisis. Suffering from an eating disorder and at war with

" AS DIANA CHARMED PEOPLE AND POLITICIANS ALIKE, IN PRIVATE SHE WAS IN CRISIS "

Lord Mountbatten and Prince Charles are pictured together just one month before the former's assassination

Margaret Thatcher arrives at 10 Downing Street after her election victory in 1979

her husband, her efforts to appeal to the Queen for understanding proved fruitless.

Although Diana was naturally shy, she quickly became a hit with the public and press in her role as Princess of Wales, and was widely celebrated as a modernising force within the royal family. The prince and princess went on many official overseas tours, including India, Canada, Nigeria, France, Japan and Austria - where Diana was photographed aboard the Concorde in April 1986. The princess also took many solo official trips overseas starting in 1982, when she represented the Queen at the state funeral of Princess Grace of Monaco, as well as trips to locations such as Norway, Germany, Nepal, Belgium and a crowd-pleasing solo trip to New York.

Despite their outward appearance as a happy couple, after five years of marriage Charles and Diana were becoming increasingly divided and unhappy, with both starting extramarital affairs. Even while he had been dating Diana, Charles was still in love with his former girlfriend, Camilla, who had married Andrew Parker Bowles in 1973. Every triumph for Diana brought new unhappiness for Charles, who increasingly turned to Camilla's friendship for comfort. It was only a matter of time before their relationship progressed beyond platonic.

Charles and Camilla reportedly rekindled their romance in 1986, with Diana ultimately confronting the latter in 1989.

While Charles was with Camilla, Diana turned to Major James Hewitt of the Household Cavalry, who had given the princess riding lessons. Their relationship was soon exposed in the press and indeed, throughout the decade, the tabloids became increasingly invasive and hostile as they tried to get the latest hot gossip surrounding the royal family.

It seemed as though the couple were constantly in the headlines and the more popular Diana became, the more resentful Charles grew. Their marriage was beset by furious arguments and infidelity on both sides, and they suffered a further blow in 1988, this time from a natural disaster. The couple were on a skiing holiday in Klosters, Switzerland, when an avalanche occurred. Their friend, Major High Lindsay, was killed, but their shared grief did nothing to bring the couple any closer together.

By now, the Queen and Duke of Edinburgh were very much aware of tensions in the marriage of Charles and Diana and held make-or-break talks to try and head off disaster. Despite their best efforts, however, the couple returned to their respective lovers. It would prove to be only a matter of time before their mutual secrets led to the breakdown of the marriage of the Prince and Princess of Wales, and caused enormous turmoil within the royal family.

Amid her crumbling marriage, Diana dedicated herself to her charity work as the president or patron of over 100 charities. She particularly focused on charities for children, the disabled, the homeless and people with HIV and AIDS. In April 1987, the princess opened the first HIV/AIDS unit at London Middlesex Hospital, where she was famously photographed shaking hands with an AIDS patient without her glove on. She was horrified to learn that children living with HIV and AIDS were often rejected by families seeking to adopt, because they were afraid of the disease. During a visit to Harlem Hospital, the Princess of Wales met children with HIV and AIDS. She spent time on the ward in New York playing with them, holding hands and, perhaps most famously, hugging them. By doing so, Diana publicly challenged the belief that the virus could be passed on through physical touch, at a time when there was a lot of misinformation and scaremongering about HIV in the media.

In June 1987, Thatcher made history once again when she was re-elected for a third term with a majority of 102 seats. This historic victory meant that she would become the longest-serving prime minister Britain had had in over 150 years, a record that is still unbroken today. In the final years of her premiership, Thatcher drew a lot of scrutiny over her attitude towards the racist apartheid regime in South Africa. Throughout the 1980s, she pursued "constructive engagement" with the white minority government to bring about change.

Although she opposed apartheid, Thatcher refused to impose the sanctions that other Western nations had implemented, believing that they were a crime against free trade. In October

The famous photograph of Diana shaking hands with an AIDS patient without gloves

Charles and Diana pose for pictures following the announcement of their engagement

Gillian Anderson stars in the latest series as Margaret Thatcher, the UK's first female prime minister

WHAT SEASON FOUR MISSED

In a decade packed with incident, *The Crown* missed out some big moments

The 1980s was a tumultuous decade and it's little wonder that *The Crown* couldn't cover everything. Two events in particular were missed, and they shook the monarchy, government and nation alike.

In June 1981, 17-year-old Marcus Sarjeant fired six blank shots at the Queen while she rode down The Mall for the annual Trooping the Colour ceremony. The Queen was unharmed and although her horse was initially spooked, she remained calm and managed to get him back under control. When Sarjeant was arrested and questioned, he claimed that he wanted to become famous, having been inspired by the assassination of John Lennon seven months prior, as well as the attempted assassinations of Ronald Reagan and Pope John Paul II.

Violence touched the country again on 12 October 1984, when Thatcher and her cabinet survived an assassination attempt by the Provisional IRA at the Grand Brighton Hotel in Brighton. They had been staying at the hotel for the Conservative Party conference and Thatcher was still awake when the bomb detonated at approximately 2.54am. Neither Thatcher nor her husband, Dennis, were injured but sadly five people who were associated with the Conservatives – including an MP – were killed and several more were left permanently disabled.

1987, she landed in hot water when she declared the African National Congress, led by an imprisoned Nelson Mandela, a "typical terrorist organisation." Still, Thatcher repeatedly urged South Africa's president, PW Botha, to release Mandela and after 27 years, he was finally freed on 11 February 1990. Even so, Thatcher's policy towards apartheid remains a controversial part of her legacy.

Thatcher was the Queen's eighth prime minister - they were in unique positions as two women in male-dominated spheres - and she was only six months older than Queen Elizabeth II. So what was their personal relationship like? The Queen and Thatcher never publicly spoke about their relationship and so it can only be speculated about. Still, it is believed that the two women were tense and awkward with each other, clashing over issues including the Falklands War and the miners' strike.

This is most evident when it came to the Commonwealth. It was clear by 1986 that the Queen was upset with tensions in the Commonwealth, the political association of which she was the head, caused by Thatcher's ambivalence to the apartheid in South Africa. That July, the Queen's press secretary told the *Sunday Times* that she found the prime minister 'uncaring' with a 'socially divisive' policy. Monarchs are not supposed to involve themselves in politics and the Queen was mortified, calling Thatcher to apologise. Nonetheless, it is said that Thatcher never forgot the Queen's criticism.

Despite the rumoured tensions between the two women, the Queen did attend Thatcher's 70th and 80th birthday celebrations, even though she was

not duty-bound. She even made Thatcher a Lady of the Garter in 1995, an honour that is usually bestowed to former prime ministers but is by no means a guarantee.

When Thatcher died in April 2013, the Queen chose to attend the funeral, marking only the second time she went to a funeral of one of her former prime ministers, with the first being Winston Churchill, her first prime minister, in 1965. Thatcher was given a ceremonial funeral, with the Queen's assent, and there were no rules to state whether the Queen had to attend or not. So, her decision to go, along with the Duke of Edinburgh, was a personal one and it demonstrated her respect for Thatcher.

In March 1990, the Conservatives announced plans for a 'poll tax' that would begin in England and Wales on 1 April. The tax was strongly opposed and led to anti-poll tax rallies, as well as a march in London, comprising 70,000 people, that ultimately led to rioting in Trafalgar Square. Her support of the poll tax, as well as her anti-EU views, sparked a crisis in confidence in Thatcher's leadership and opposition from her own party. The woman who had seemed unassailable just ten years earlier was now under attack from those who had once been her strongest supporters. The Thatcherite era was over.

Thatcher resigned as prime minister and Conservative Party leader on 22 November 1990. As Britain moved into a new decade, it was a socially, politically and economically changed country from what it had been at the start of the 1980s - and for the royal family, there were challenges ahead the likes of which they could only imagine.

The Grand Hotel bombing in Brighton killed five people and injured 31 others

A HOUSE AND COUNTRY DIVIDED

The 1990s found a couple at war, a country in turmoil and a queen under fire

Words by **Catherine Curzon**

If the 1980s had been tumultuous, the decade that followed saw the monarchy under the most intense scrutiny it had faced for years. With marriages collapsing like a house of cards and Windsor Castle facing a catastrophic fate, it was little wonder that Queen Elizabeth II declared 1992 her "annus horribilis". For the government, things were little better. While John Major was settling in to 10 Downing Street, he found himself assailed by the fallout from Margaret Thatcher's poll tax, as well as challenges from home and abroad that saw the country go to war and the once seemingly unassailable Tory government fall.

In 1992, the royal family saw the collapse of not one but three of its children's marriages. The Duke and Duchess of York's separation was preceded by revelations regarding the duchess's private life and the couple announced their split in March. A month later, Princess Anne and her husband, Captain Mark Phillips, were divorced after a separation of three years. Far more notorious and damaging to the family was, of course, the breakdown of the marriage between Charles and Diana, the Prince and Princess of Wales.

The state of the Wales' marriage had long been the subject of speculation in the media as the couple appeared increasingly distant from one another, and rumours of affairs on both sides were rife. Charles had returned to his affair with Camilla Parker Bowles, while Diana's five-year relationship with James Hewitt, her riding instructor, had ended in 1991. The first public acknowledgement of very real problems in the couple's marriage came with the publication of Andrew Morton's explosive book *Diana: Her True*

Story in May 1992. Though Diana's intimate involvement in the book wasn't revealed until after her death, its publication caused a sensation. Filled with revelations regarding Charles's relationship with Camilla Parker Bowles - while omitting any mention of the princess's own love affairs - and revealing Diana's struggles with her mental health, as well as claiming that her husband drove her to attempt suicide, it was the first time the public had seen anything like it. As the full glare of the spotlight turned on the couple, both the prince and princess found their telephones bugged and intimate conversations between them and their extramarital partners splashed across the front pages. Readers could even ring a premium rate number to listen to the tapes themselves, if the transcripts weren't salacious enough.

As the royal marriages crumbled, 1992 still had one last unfortunate ace to play on the House of Windsor. At 11.15am on 20 November 1992, a fire broke out in the Queen's Private Chapel at Windsor Castle, where a spotlight had caused a curtain to ignite. As the blaze spread, the fire brigade battled for more than 12 hours to get the flames under control. By the time they were finally doused by 1.5 million gallons of water, large parts of the castle lay in ruins. Ironically, the value of the items in the Royal Collection and the castle itself made them too valuable to insure, and it was eventually decided that the repair costs would be met by a combination of £2 million from the Queen, donations made to a restoration trust and the introduction of an entry fee to visit Windsor Castle and Buckingham Palace. As part of this plan, the Queen agreed to begin paying income

Tony Blair's Labour Party swept to government in 1997 on a landslide

tax. She was the first British monarch to do so in six decades.

It was little wonder that when Queen Elizabeth II made a speech in honour of her Ruby Jubilee on 24 November, she described 1992 as her "annus horribilis", but the year had one final unpleasant ace to play. On 9 December, Prime Minister John Major announced that the Prince and Princess of Wales would separate, ending speculation once and for all. Major assured the public that the separation was amicable, but behind closed doors it was all-out war.

John Major's announcement regarding the marriage of the Prince and Princess of Wales came little more than two years after he had succeeded Margaret Thatcher as prime minister. After 11 years of Thatcherism, public trust in the Conservative Party was low, but Major hoped to turn its fortunes around. Unlike Thatcher, who famously claimed that there was "no such thing as society", John Major pledged to build a "classless society" and he followed through on his pledge to review the incendiary poll tax, which was abolished in 1991. Two years later it was replaced by the council tax.

Though the early months of Major's premiership were dominated by economic issues and rising unemployment, perhaps the most immediate issue that confronted him when he came to power was the outbreak of the Gulf War. Major committed British troops to international efforts to pushback against Saddam Hussein's invasion of Kuwait, a decision that occupied the vast majority of his time and thoughts during the short conflict.

When he won the leadership of the Conservative Party, Major promised his party and the electorate a new start. He sealed his mandate with the 1992 general election, at which the Conservatives claimed an unexpected majority. What new hope Major promised, however, was forgotten by September and the economic devastation wrought on Black Wednesday, 16 September 1992. This now infamous day signified a new low in the economic fortunes of the United Kingdom. The fall of the pound forced the UK out of the European Exchange Rate Mechanism, leading to a currency crash that plunged the country into recession. Efforts to prop up the failing pound cost the Bank of England more than £3 billion in one day and Black Wednesday fatally

undermined the prime minister's apparently solid and relatively low-risk economic policy.

John Major's other campaigns fared little better, especially the much-trumpeted Back to Basics movement, which was intended to instil traditional social values. Instead, the announcement of the Back to Basics strategy was swiftly followed by a lurid avalanche of scandals at the top of government, with ministers and Members of Parliament coming under fire for everything from sexual indiscretion to fraud and insider-dealing.

As the Conservative government reeled with scandal, Major hoped to bring the focus back onto parliamentary affairs. He presided over the privatisation of British Rail, a long drawn-out process under which the national rail network was sold off to private companies. This was a hugely controversial decision that seemed to cause as many new issues as it resolved, and plunged the tottering Conservative government into a new round of trouble.

If John Major had been hoping for something to draw the attention of the public and press away from his own political struggles, he was granted it in the acrimonious turn that the royal separation was taking. With their broken marriage under more intense scrutiny than ever, Charles and Diana's moves were watched, analysed and evaluated. In an effort to undo some of the damage done by *Diana: Her True Story*, Charles agreed to take part in a documentary entitled *Charles: The Private Man, the Public Role*. For the first time he admitted that he had committed adultery with a nameless party, claiming that he had done so only when it was clear to both he and Diana that the marriage was beyond saving.

In giving the interview, Charles had hoped to put his case honestly, rather than via subterfuge and leaks to friendly journalists. Aware of public affection for his wife, who was seen as a sympathetic figure in contrast to his own somewhat dour, patrician image, Charles had hoped that he could redress the balance and show himself not as a remote, uncaring figure, but as a human being. To some extent he succeeded, but he also divided the nation down the middle,

The First Gulf War of 1991 got John Major's premiership off to a challenging start

"MAJOR ASSURED THE PUBLIC THAT THE SEPARATION WAS AMICABLE, BUT BEHIND CLOSED DOORS IT WAS ALL-OUT WAR"

The Queen and Prince Philip look over some of the tributes left outside Buckingham Palace following Princess Diana's death in 1997

leading to heated debate on whether he was suited to be monarch at all.

As the future of the monarchy and Charles's behaviour remained a hot topic, Princess Diana appeared to be going from strength to strength. Charles's admission saw her receive even more public sympathy but it also left her determined to tell her side of the story. Though it was revealed after her death that she had collaborated with Morton on his explosive book, there was no attempt to hide her involvement in the by now notorious *Panorama* interview that had such an impact on public consciousness. An audience of 200 million people across the world eventually saw the broadcast of 20 November 1995, in which Martin Bashir interviewed the princess. Diana discussed candidly the breakdown of her marriage, presenting her husband as an unsympathetic and uncaring man whose behaviour led her to self-harm and become bulimic. The bombshell came when she broached the issue of Camilla Parker Bowles, saying famously "there were three of us in this marriage", and bringing the full glare of the spotlight onto her apparent rival. The princess spoke about the media pressure she was under and the lack of affection and understanding that she had received from the wider royal family, which appeared outdated and cold. *Panorama: An Interview with HRH The Princess of Wales* changed the way the media and public viewed the royal family forever and cemented the image of Diana as the grievously wronged party across the world.

In 2020 it emerged that Bashir had gone to extreme and dishonest lengths to secure the interview, including forging bank statements in order to win Diana's trust. An independent enquiry later found him guilty of breaching BBC editorial conduct and deceit in order to land the interview.

Panorama sealed the fate of the couple's marriage once and for all. The Queen advised Charles and Diana to divorce but, as the negotiations were going on, Diana accused the couple's former nanny of having aborted Charles's baby. Her behaviour caused consternation at Buckingham Palace, who were unaware that the false abortion story had been fostered by Bashir during his communication with the princess. The couple's divorce was finalised on 18 August 1996, and Diana was stripped of her HRH status. Instead, she would be known as Diana, Princess of Wales.

The country had never seen anything quite like the outpouring of grief for Diana

On 1 May 1997, a general election finally put the Conservative government out of its misery. John Major's party was defeated by a landslide and Tony Blair's Labour government swept to power with a 179-seat majority, including a gain of 146 seats. The new Labour administration promised a fresh and honest start, offering optimism, growth and open government. It was the dawn of the so-called Cool Britannia era, but the new government's early promise was not to last forever.

Perhaps ironically, given how she had spoken of the pressure of media attention, Diana's romantic life continued to fascinate royal-

The Queen faced a devastating blow when fire raged through Windsor Castle

watchers across the globe. In 1995 she began dating Hasnat Khan, a British-Pakistani surgeon whom Diana is said to have called "the love of her life". The couple were together for two years, during which time Diana travelled to Lahore to meet Khan's family. Despite the opposition of Khan's parents, speculation began to mount that a marriage might lay in their future but ultimately, Khan found the press attention too much to bear. The relationship ended in summer 1997, leaving Diana heartbroken.

A month after the end of her relationship with Hasnat Khan, Diana began dating Dodi Fayed, the son of Harrods owner Mohamed Al-Fayed. After spending time with Al-Fayed's family in the South of France, Diana and Dodi Fayed travelled together to Paris. On 31 August 1997, Diana and Dodi were killed in a car crash in the Pont de l'Alma tunnel in Paris, while being pursued by the paparazzi. Their driver, Henri Paul, also died in the wreck.

The death of Diana, Princess of Wales, plunged the nation and the world into mourning. One person who certainly judged the public mood correctly was Tony Blair. Never short of a soundbite, when he stood before television cameras on the morning of Diana's death and paid tribute to "the People's Princess", he coined a phrase that would be forever associated with Diana. The United Kingdom had never seen anything quite like it and as crowds gathered at Buckingham Palace and hundreds of thousands of bouquets and offerings were left at royal sites across the country, the public had only one question: where was the Queen?

Queen Elizabeth II's absence during the days immediately after Diana's death led to accusations that she was a monster, incapable of showing normal human emotion. As the monarchy itself seemed under threat, the reality was that the Queen was actually caring for her grandsons, putting her duties as a grandmother ahead of those of a sovereign. Yet, as public opinion increasingly turned against the royal family, Elizabeth realised that she must take action. She made a live television broadcast in tribute to her former daughter-in-law and went to view the tributes and meet mourners at royal palaces across London. Eventually the Royal Standard over Buckingham Palace, which wasn't flying at half-mast due to protocol, was replaced by a Union Flag at half-mast. It was the start of a significant modernisation of the monarchy.

Diana, Princess of Wales, was laid to rest on 6 September 1997 in front of a television audience estimated at 2.5 billion. The immense pageantry of her funeral was brought into sharp focus by scenes of her young sons walking in procession behind the coffin of their mother, their faces etched with grief. The death of Diana closed a tumultuous chapter in the history of the British monarchy. As the world looked towards a new millennium, the House of Windsor had been changed forever.

THE NEXT CHAPTER

Fans of *The Crown* have rejoiced at confirmation of a sixth season

When season five of *The Crown* was commissioned, the good news came with a sting in the tail: this was where the story would end, and there would be no season six. Fans had cause to celebrate several months later when Netflix announced that they had changed their minds, and that there would be one more season of the show. What will feature is tightly under wraps, but the early 2000s offer no shortage of dramatic incidents both at home and in the wider world.

The Queen's response to the events of 11 September 2001 will likely play a role in the new season, as the tragedy changed the world forever. On a more personal note, Queen Elizabeth II lost both her mother and her sister, Princess Margaret, within the space of six weeks in 2002, two women who had been with her through good times and bad. Yet the decade also saw happier events, such as Prince William meeting Kate Middleton at university, as well as the Queen celebrating her Golden Jubilee. A casting call for the role of Prince William suggests that he will also be playing a significant role in the new season.

Finally, it's highly likely that viewers will finally see Prince Charles and Camilla Parker Bowles tie the knot. With the couple now King and Queen Consort, it would be too good a finale to miss.

The current King and Queen Consort at the wedding of Zara Phillips and Mike Tindall in 2011

Images © Alamy

STORY OF THE
BATTLE *of* BRITAIN

THE ROYAL NAVY
How the Home Fleet played a vital part...

EXCLUSIVE INTERVIEW SIR MAX HASTINGS

Examine world wars and epic battles through maps and rare documents

BRITAIN'S BRAVE FOREIGN FIGHTERS
Meet the pilots from overseas who took to the skies alongside the RAF

THE WAAF • INSIDE THE LUFTWAFFE • THE COST OF DEFEAT

HISTORY
ANGLO-SAXONS
DISCOVER THE RISE AND FALL OF ENGLAND'S ILL-FATED FOREFATHERS

1066

VIKING INVASION • SUTTON HOO • KING ALFRED

ANNE BOLEYN
AND THE **SIX WIVES**
At the Tudor court, lust & ambition could lead to fatal consequences...

HENRY'S LAST LOVE?

THE REFORMATION • SUCCESSION CRISIS • MISTRESSES • EXECUTIONS

STALIN
EXPLORE THE LIFE AND CRIMES OF ONE OF HISTORY'S MOST NOTORIOUS LEADERS

HITLER *vs* STALIN

RISE TO POWER • WORLD WAR II • THE GREAT PURGE • STALIN'S LEGACY

BOOK *of*
Death

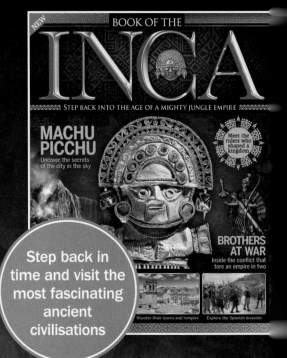

BOOK OF THE
INCA
STEP BACK INTO THE AGE OF A MIGHTY JUNGLE EMPIRE

MACHU PICCHU
Uncover the secrets of the city in the sky

Meet the rulers who shaped a kingdom

BROTHERS AT WAR
Inside the conflict that tore an empire in two

Wander their towns and temples   Explore the Spanish invasion

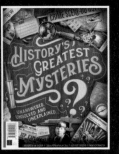

History's GREATEST MYSTERIES
UNSOLVED AND UNEXPLAINED

ANCIENT GODS
DISCOVER THE POWERFUL AND MYSTERIOUS DEITIES OF THE PAST

PLUS: MEET THE 10 STRANGEST GODS OF ANTIQUITY

HEROES *of the*
FIRST WORLD WAR

ON THE FRONT • FLYING ACES • WOMEN AT WAR • MEDALS

Step back in time and visit the most fascinating ancient civilisations

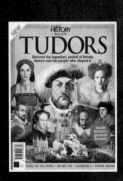

SALEM WITCH TRIALS

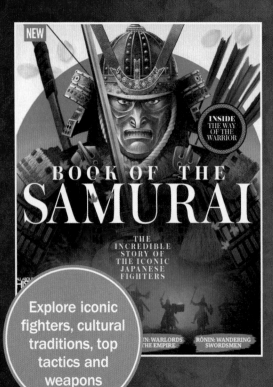

INSIDE THE WAY OF THE WARRIOR

BOOK OF THE
SAMURAI
THE INCREDIBLE STORY OF THE ICONIC JAPANESE FIGHTERS

...N: WARLORDS ...THE EMPIRE   RŌNIN: WANDERING SWORDSMEN

Explore iconic fighters, cultural traditions, top tactics and weapons

EVERYTHING YOU NEED TO KNOW ABOUT
THE
MIDDLE AGES
FROM THE FALL OF ROME TO THE RISE OF EUROPE

PLUS

DARK AGES?   HORDES & HOARDS   AGE OF CHIVALRY

AZTECS
DELVE INTO THE DEPTHS OF A MYSTERIOUS CIVILISATION

HISTORY
Book of the
TUDORS
Discover the legendary period of British history and the people who shaped it

Inside Britain's greatest dynasty

WAR OF THE ROSES • HENRY VIII • ELIZABETH I • TUDOR EMPIRE

GEORGIANS
The remarkable dynasty that oversaw the industrial revolution and a changing Britain

THE FALL OF EMPIRES

HERETICS HOLY WAR

RECONQUISTA • THE CRUSADES • EIGHTY YEAR...

Get great savings when you buy direct from us

1000s of great titles, many not available anywhere else

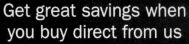

World-wide delivery an... super-safe ordering

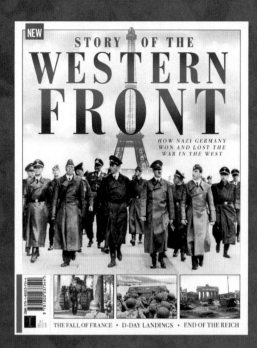

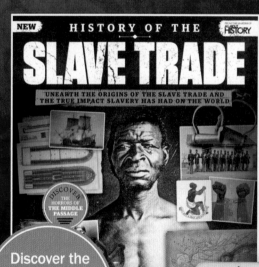

SEASON 5 IS HERE

Catch up on the previous seasons of the groundbreaking royal drama, go behind the scenes and explore its sets, locations and costumes, find out why its storylines continue to stoke controversy, and get ready to enjoy the latest season of The Crown.

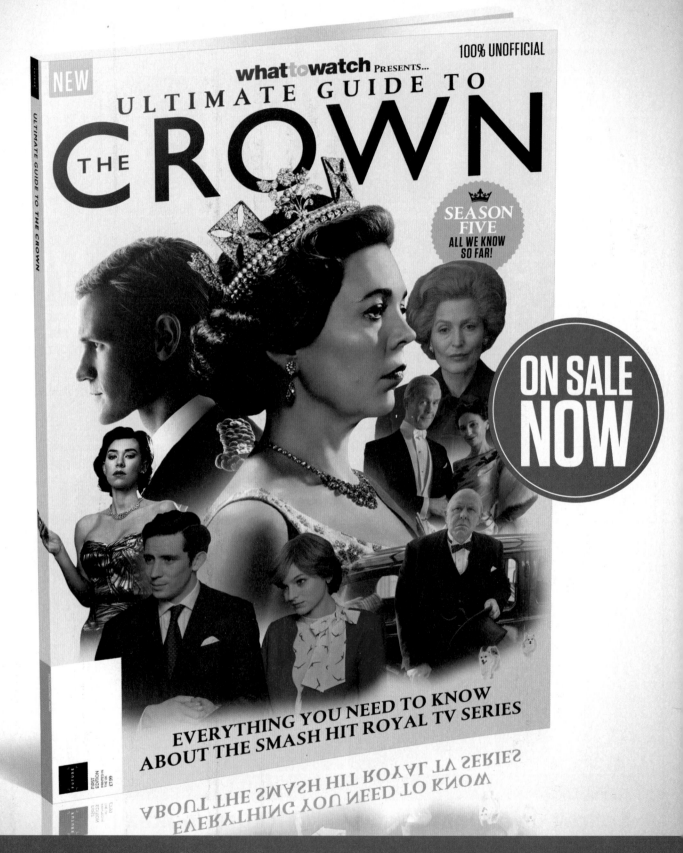